Betty & Ke...

Thank you so...
for your hospitality

the 500 hats
of a
Modern-Day
woman

I really appreciate
your ministry & gift!

God bless you.

Love ya bunches ♡
Janine

the 500 hats
of a
Modern-Day
woman

Strength for Today's
Demanding Roles

Joyce K. Ellis

VINE BOOKS

SERVANT PUBLICATIONS
ANN ARBOR, MICHIGAN

Vine Books is an imprint of Servant Publications especially designed to serve evangelical Christians.

All Scripture quotations not marked otherwise are from the HOLY BIBLE, NEW INTERNATIONAL VERSION. Copyright 1973, 1978, International Bible Society. Used by permission of Zondervan Bible Publishers. All rights reserved.

Portions of chapter 3 originally appeared as "Heresy in Counted Cross-Stitch" by Joyce K. Ellis in *Woman's Touch*, May/June 1986.
Portions of chapter 4 originally appeared as "Stay at Home or Go to Work? How Does a Mother Decide?" by Joyce K. Ellis in *Lookout*, August 4, 1996.
The poem "After the Stroke" by Joyce K. Ellis in chapter 5 originally appeared in *Scope*, August 1979.

Note: Names have been changed in some anecdotes to protect individuals in sensitive situations.

Published by Servant Publications
P.O. Box 8617
Ann Arbor, Michigan 48107

Cover photograph: Bob Foran, Ann Arbor, MI

98 99 00 01 10 9 8 7 6 5 4 3 2 1

Printed in the United States of America
ISBN 1-56955-064-6

Library of Congress Cataloging-in-Publication Data

Ellis, Joyce K.
The 500 hats of a modern-day woman : strength for today's demanding roles / Joyce K. Ellis.
    p.   cm. — (Women of confidence series)
Includes bibliographical references.
ISBN 1-56955-064-6 (alk. paper)
1. Christian women—Religious life.   I. Title.   II. Title: Five hundred hats of a modern-day woman.   III. Series.
BV4527.E45   1999
248.8'43—dc21   98-47458
                                                       CIP

Dedication

This book is lovingly dedicated to

my daughters Sharie and Maryanne,
and my daughter-in-law, Heather,
with the prayer that you will look to Christ more and more to
balance your growing roles as young women

and to Missy and Terri,
with the same prayer and immense gratitude for encouraging
me to "go for it" when I first contemplated writing this book.

Contents

Acknowledgments 9

About the Study Questions 11

Introduction: Bartholomew Cubbins and Me 13

1. Is My Picture Hat Worthy of a Kodak Moment? 17
   My Role as a Woman

2. Does That Wedding Veil Still Fit? 37
   My Role as a Wife

3. Has Anyone Seen My Chauffeur's Cap? 51
   My Role as a Mother, Need-Meeter, Nurturer, et al.

4. Why Didn't They Tell Me Hard Hats Must Be Worn in
   This Area? 71
   My Role as a Working Woman (at Home or Abroad)

5. Caroline Ingalls, Will You Tie My Sunbonnet? 95
   My Role as a Daughter (and Daughter-in-Law)

6. Is My Halo On Straight? 119
   My Role in God's Family

7. Why Does My Maid's Cap Keep Slipping? 145
   My Role as Servant of All

8. Who Gives Out the Pith Helmets? 167
   My Role as an Adventurer in God's Kingdom

9. Does a Black Veil Go With Everything? 187
   My Role in Aging Gracefully

10. Will You P-l-ease Let Me in Front of the Mirror? . . .205
    How Do I View My Many Hats?

Acknowledgments

My thanks to Dr. Seuss for his charming book, *The 500 Hats of Bartholomew Cubbins,* the inspiration and springboard for this material.

Thanks to all the women across the country who, in some cases, took hours to complete my survey about their many roles. Without your honesty, insights, stories, prayers, and encouragement, this project would have been impossible.

Thanks to my parents, Ed and Eunice Krohne, who always believed in me and instilled a healthy view of my femininity.

Thanks to my daughter Sharie for her encouragement, typing up notes, and support help throughout this long process. Your periodic admonitions to "Get to work on your book, Mom" helped more than you'll ever know.

Thanks to my critique group—Lois, Alice, Pam, and Sharon—for your faithfulness in helping me polish my manuscript and keeping me on task. Your kudos and criticisms saved me embarrassment and strengthened the final product. We've been together a lot of years, and I can never repay you for all you've done for me.

Thanks to Bonnie Stedman, my prayer partner through much of this project. You have no idea what your prayer support and encouragement have meant to me! I trust God will bless you in a special way for the part you've played in making this book a reality.

Thanks to Linda Linder, who came into my life again at a most opportune time. Your friendship and prayers have encouraged me greatly.

Thanks to Gwen Ellis (no relation), my initial editor, who laughed in the right spots when she read my first chapter and encouraged me until I finished the manuscript. Your quiet confidence in me kept me writing when I thought I'd never get this book done.

Thanks to Kathy Deering, the personification of her title as Servant editor, who became my late-inning cheerleader and reminded me that overwhelming tasks can be broken into smaller ones, prioritized, and completed.

A belated thanks to my grandmother Lois Eugenia Harrison Ostertag, now in heaven, who saw and encouraged God's gifts in me many years ago. Many of her unforgettable words of wisdom and great humor begged to be included in this book. I couldn't keep them to myself.

Special thanks to my loving, supportive husband, Steve, who often sacrifices much so I can write. Your encouragement—and needling when necessary—always helped me keep the end in sight, and your prayers helped me get there. I love you so much.

And most important, thanks to my Creator, who has helped me get to know Him and myself better through this project. Without You, Lord, I know I can do nothing. But with You anything is possible!

Soli Deo Gloria!

About the Study Questions

When the women in our church learned about this book-in-progress, they asked me to adapt the material for our women's Bible study. It was a challenge, but I found that *The 500 Hats of a Modern-Day Woman* lends itself well to a ten-week study—a lighter study suitable even for women who have never attended a Bible study before.

The questions at the end of each chapter dig a little deeper into the Scriptures presented in that chapter, examine other relevant passages, and call for personal reflection and application. You may photocopy these for your group's use if you leave the copyright designation on them.

The questions at the end of chapter 1 can be discussed at the first session without prior preparation. But thereafter, we would encourage each participant to first answer the study questions at the end of the chapter and *then* read the chapter before meeting together to discuss what you have learned each week. It's better to "dig" on your own first.

May God encourage your hearts through this material!

Joyce K. Ellis

Introduction

Bartholomew Cubbins and Me

Maybe you remember the Dr. Seuss story *The 500 Hats of Bartholomew Cubbins*,[1] based on an old English fairy tale. That poor little fellow only wanted to see the king but was sent to the dungeon for not taking off his hat when the king's coach passed by. Actually Bartholomew *had* taken off his hat, but as soon as he took it off, another hat instantly appeared in its place. As he doffed that one, another and another appeared. And each looked exactly like the one before—a plain little hat with one feather sticking out.

Of course the king grew more and more furious as the insolence continued. Through various events that day, including his nearly being beheaded, Bartholomew kept trying to get rid of the hats—but he couldn't. One after another they flew off his head, littering the streets, the palace steps, and even the throne room.

But then, at the 451st hat, things began to change. The hats weren't plain anymore. They began to sprout feathers and display jewels—each hat more beautiful than the one before—until at last, the 500th was the most spectacular of all.

In fact, the king was so enthralled with the fabulous 500th hat that he decided he must have it, and he bought it from the boy on the spot. When Bartholomew lifted the 500th hat from his head to give it to the king, he felt a refreshing and liberating breeze blowing through his hair. Finally rid of all the hats, Bartholomew's head was bare.

It's a fanciful story, but Bartholomew's plight reminds me a great deal of our lives as women. How many hats we wear! And what quick-change artists we have become! As quickly as we take one hat off, another appears in its place. And it sometimes seems as though we will never again feel a carefree breeze blowing through our hair.

But unlike Bartholomew's hats, each one of our hats differs from the next. And few are plain!

When a hat is new, it fills us with excitement and joy. Nothing compares to the feeling of wearing a new hat—being a new bride, a new mom, a new worker in our chosen field. We feel so smartly dressed and hold our heads just so. Our posture improves. We're certain that every eye in the room is on us. What confidence!

But then our lovely new hats get knocked around a bit. Wrinkles and dents leave once-crisp shapes limp and lopsided. Dust and dirt and greasy fingerprints dull the vibrant colors. Frustration, worry, and dungeons (sometimes of our own making) may replace our earlier feelings of fulfillment and importance.

As we add more hats, they often become not more fabulous but more dilapidated. And there isn't a king anywhere who would pay us two cents to take them off our hands.

So how do we view our hats—our many diverse roles? And how do we find strength and maintain balance under the leaning tower precariously perched atop our heads? I hope you enjoy this trip through our fanciful millinery shop. Even if you come across a chapter dealing with a hat you don't wear, I hope you'll read through the chapter anyway. Perhaps it will give you some insights into the challenges and joys of those around you who do wear that hat.

Please join me in front of the changing room mirror on the pages that follow as some friends and I evaluate how our hats are fitting and chat about the design, style, and presence of our own 500 (more or less) hats.

ONE

Is My Picture Hat Worthy of a Kodak Moment?

My Role as a Woman

I like the fact that I'm a complex, emotional being who feels life intensely.

—Colleen Watson
Her hats include those of a licensed
practical nurse, songwriter,
wife of a family therapist,
mother of two young adults.

My mother-in-law always laughed when she saw a bright orange "Men Working" highway sign. "When women work, that's nothing new," she quipped, "but when men work, they put up a sign!" Of course, her razzing always provoked a corresponding female put-down from some incensed male within listening distance.

But sign or no sign, women do work hard; sometimes we complain about all the hats we have to juggle—beginning with simply being a woman.

The large-brimmed picture hat of yesteryear daintily framed a woman's face, drawing attention to the loveliness of her femininity. I'll admit to days when I feel like stomping all over my feminine hat, but I don't think most of us would trade our gender even if God threw in a coupon good for five extra hours in a day. For one thing, we wouldn't use those extra hours for rest. We'd cram in more work and more activities, which would only leave us more exhausted.

While we happily enjoy our ingenious labor-saving devices and the freedom to do and be anything we want (at least theoretically), many of us reach for more. And, indeed, we find more—more work and more stress. Unlike our "foremothers," we don't churn our own high-cholesterol spread or slap the perspiration stains out of our clothes on a corrugated metal washboard. But with so much extra time left over (Ha!)—since we don't have to do those pioneer-era chores—other expectations vacuum the energy right out of us.

Perpetual Wipe Out

When my kids were little, I used to think that only mothers of small children or mothers who worked outside the home dragged through life in perpetual "wipe out." But I've since learned differently. Several months ago I sent an extensive survey to about a hundred women of all ages across the country, asking for input about their roles and attitudes, their joys and struggles.

Of course some were too busy juggling their hats to complete the survey. But many did respond. And whether single, married, divorced, or widowed, nearly all talked about the difficulty of maintaining energy levels in the midst of responsibility.

A single woman nearing retirement said the most difficult parts of being a working woman are "getting up too early, having to wear pantyhose, and not having much time left for family and friends." That about sums it up, doesn't it? Unless you happen to be a morning person.

I am so grateful that in my most recent office job (after more than twenty years away from the corporate work environment) my boss's body clock ran in the same time zone as mine. (She wasn't a morning person either.) So I didn't have to be at the office until 9 A.M. But for about a year I had to carpool with my husband, who dropped me off promptly at 7:30—a time I barely knew existed in the A.M.

Fortunately, my office had a door I could close. So on occasion—OK, on many occasions—I would lie on the floor, carefully smooth my skirt beneath me, plop my needlepointed pillow beneath my head, and throw my suit jacket over me for a nice, warm, extra snooze before the workday began. Or sometimes I'd nap during that post-lunch drowsy time when most sane countries insist their employees take corporately sanctioned siestas.

Whether or not we work outside the home, I'm convinced that learning to manage energy levels is a lifelong process. Each stage of life, each new child, each new community responsibility, each new job change, requires us to haul out the balance scales. Now that our options are so much greater than were our grandmothers', we often must decide between two or more *great* opportunities.

My grandmother, I'm sure, would cluck her tongue at my often less-than-tidy house with its accompanying fine-to-medium layer of dust. Isn't housework the first thing most of us let go? But I think Grandma would also smile warmly at some of the opportunities I've had. And she would be my number-one encourager.

Gains and Losses

Our many opportunities today as women can make us so tired and so confused that we can actually become less fulfilled if we're not careful. In her book *Have We Really Come a Long Way?* Ruth Senter says that with all our accomplishments and advances you'd think we would find more contentment. But instead we see a deepening discontent. "Always another peak to conquer.... Not quite enough. There's more...."

"Maybe our freedom has become our ball and chain," Senter says. "Maybe the more we gain, the more gains we want. Maybe ... somewhere along the way we lost some of the priceless commodities we had." She names lovely qualities like sensitivity, humor, sisterhood, reflection, dreaming, and hope.[1]

The more women have melded with the macho spirit of the workplace and the community, the more phrases like *setting priorities, time management,* and *you'll always find time for what you really want to do* burrow their way into our mindset. Personally, I've heard that last cliché from people who (among other things) thought I should sell Amway, exercise more, spend more time writing, spend more time reading, pursue more academic goals, volunteer for their organizations, or become more spiritual—however *they* defined spirituality.

But it's not true that you'll always find time for what you really want to do. I really want to do too many things. There simply are not enough hours in the day, days in a year, or years in a lifetime to do them all. Life is exciting! There's so much to learn, to see, to do.

So I, myself, have proclaimed the same maxims I chafe under. With so much we *have* to do and so much we *want* to do, it makes sense to pay attention to priorities, work efficiently, and try to make wise choices. But a woman's heart longs for the softer side—some key elements that can unlock the clunky, rigid ball and chain. Here are a few I'm working on:

1. *More isn't always better.* Most of us know that if we're taking medication, we need to take the prescribed amount. More could actually kill us. Yet sometimes, when it comes to feeling fulfilled, we look at how busy we are or how far up the ladder we've climbed rather than whether we're enjoying where we are.

Why do we knock ourselves out to keep up with the Joanies? or Shandras? or Lindseys? Each of us is a unique creation with specific needs, desires, and thresholds of excitement. If we look to our Creator, He can help us appreciate our unique womanhood and guide us in determining what we can handle. That's what this book is about.

2. *Choose people over projects.* A TV commercial advertising cellular phones taps into our guilt. The kids can't go to the beach because Mom has a meeting with a client. So the youngest child pouts and says in that cute little voice no mother could resist, "Mommy, when do I get to be the client?" The ultimate solution to all life's problems, according to the commercial, is another appendage—the cellular phone, which allows Mom to meet with her client while she frolics in the sun with her cherubs on the beach. But of course the cell phone perpetually stuck to her hip also gives her no true time off.

Women are generally more nurturing and relational than men. We all know that. So we're chaining ourselves to false perceptions when we try to deny our relational side. Schedules are important. But like rules, they're made to be broken—sometimes. A brief chat in the ladies' room is as good as eight ounces of caffeine—hot or cold—to pick us up in the afternoon at the office. We can actually work more efficiently at our housework after a five-minute phone call to a friend or relative. We've connected. We're not alone.

When my husband and I were planning our wedding, more than a quarter of a century ago, he taught me how to make lists and check off each item as completed so I could untangle the huge knot of details. Over the years, as a wife and mother, I found this list thing quite helpful, especially when the kids were little and it seemed I never got anything done. Sometimes one check mark on a day's to-do list merited a major celebration!

Interruptions can drive us crazy, both at home and at work, but allowing time for nurturing and relating can bring better perspective to our lives.

Maybe I didn't get all my housework done every day, but my kids will never forget my showing them how to make a tent out of blankets thrown over the Ping-Pong table in the basement, or teaching them to read, or making them forget their momentary traumas with a kiss and the simple question, "Do you think you'll live till next Tuesday?" (Just a day I picked out of the air. Nothing particularly important going on then.)

Maybe you had to come to work early or stay late once or twice to meet your deadline, but your coworker will never forget your sitting and compassionately listening to her struggles with her boss. A single friend told me that although she probably never will have any children of her own, she enjoys "mothering" other people's kids and even her own peers at work. Nurturing comes naturally for us. Why not enjoy it?

3. *Choose being over doing.* As a unique creation of God, we are each significant simply because He made us. We don't have to *try* to become significant or *prove* our significance by doing something extraordinary or measuring up to someone else's definition of success. How freeing it is to know my Creator put me in this place, at this time, for His own reasons. So I can be comfortable with who I am.

Because we have so many opportunities today, we may feel we've not met our potential if we don't reach the supposed prestigious positions—astronaut, CEO, or research scientist discovering a cure for some heinous disease. But if God—who is all-wise and never makes a mistake—designed me to be a hospital volunteer, nose-wiper in my own home day-care, or tour guide at the local zoo, then that is the perfect position for me. I'd be miserable in a space suit, business attire, or a lab coat.

We don't have to limit our dreams. But it's also good to remember that feeling satisfied and fulfilled doesn't depend on the title on our door, the size of our paycheck, or the height of our rung on the ladder.

We can't afford to deny who we are to prove a point.

All Things Anatomical and Emotional

On a recent business trip I shared a hotel room with a female colleague young enough to be my daughter. One morning she awoke in pain, grumbling about her mother's admonitions to be happy about this wonderful monthly blessing that would enable her to one day bring another life into the world. "Yippee," she droned.

As my grandmother used to say, "I've been there and spent the day."

I honestly believe that God, our Creator, knows all things and is all-powerful. So I am sure that if there were a better way for our bodies to be prepared to bear the one or two or more little rascals some of us were called to bring into this world, He would have thought of it (that little curse thing in the Garden of Eden notwithstanding). But I admit I shake my head in bewilderment.

I feel the same way about my emotional makeup. You know how some people wear their emotions on their sleeves? I wear mine all over my face and down my blouse. I trace my history of easy-weeping eyes through generations of television shows: *Lassie; Marcus Welby, M.D.; Little House on the Prairie;* and now *E.R.*—and let's not forget those Kodak-moment commercials. All dress rehearsals for big-time moments of grief like losing my dear brother-in-law, my mother-in-law, a close friend of more than twenty years, and finally a job that was my "heart"—all within a few years.

When I lost my job, I learned about the downsizing the Thursday before a holiday weekend. My boss asked me not to tell anyone at the office because the powers-that-be wanted to explain the situation at a full staff meeting when everyone returned on Tuesday. Grateful that I didn't work Fridays, I went back to my office, had a good cry behind my closed door, and tried to figure out how to interact with people before Tuesday without blubbering my way through the conversation. I made arrangements to work at home the rest of the day and quickly slipped out of the building undetected.

It's so embarrassing to be emotional! From the time my kids were little, when we watched a sad show together, they'd peek over at me to see if any little tears had escaped yet. Often I'd take a bathroom break whether I needed it or not, just for a chance to wipe my eyes. Still today if we go to a movie theater, my husband graciously sits through all the credits with me to give my face a chance to return to flesh tone after it's been ruby-red through the sad parts of the film. I used to hate my tears—still do, sometimes. But I'm learning to respect them.

Sometimes we *need* tears. One night my husband and I came home and found our twenty-something daughter snuggled in a warm bathrobe in the recliner with tears streaming down her face. Imagining some great catastrophe, we asked her what was wrong. "Oh, I just got home from work and needed a good Disney cry," she said. *The Fox and the Hound* did the trick, and she was fine. Men will never understand that!

Maybe you're not as emotional as the women in my family. But perhaps you can identify with the joke: "How many women with PMS does it take to change a light bulb?" Answer (shouted at the top of one's lungs): "Who wants to know?" Our emotions and hormones often leave us feeling out of control, but I try to remember that's a *reason,* not an *excuse,* for "women behaving badly." We need a lot of grace to apologize freely or, better yet, take our own "time out" to regain control so we don't hurt those we love most.

God made the heart of a woman tender—beautifully tender. We can feel deeply with one another and with the men in our lives. We can put ourselves in another person's place and experience that person's joys and sorrows. We can encourage and help others because we can "feel" with them, not just fire off cannons with flags that say, "Buck up," or, "It'll all work out." God gave us this gift of tenderness and sisterhood. It is a reflection of His own compassion and gentleness that we should prize and nurture.

The Married-Single Sidestep

A number of years ago, comedian George Carlin did a monologue about things we don't have a word for in the English language. For example, while walking down the street, you meet a man walking toward you, directly in your path. Simultaneously, you take a step to your right, and he takes a step to his left. So you're facing each other again. You try another sidestep only to find him moving in the same direction. We all know the off-balance feeling, the uncertainty, the frustration. "There ought to be a word for that," Carlin says.

Yes, there should, because then I'd have a better subtitle for this section. I sometimes think the sidewalk two-step—may I coin the term?—describes rather well the little dance that sometimes goes on between single women and married women. If sisterhood is indeed worth developing, it seems we need better tools for relating to one another. Sometimes, I think, we're so worried about saying the wrong thing or offending someone that we avoid making friendships with those whose marital status differs from ours.

Because I was nineteen when I got married and almost twenty-one when our first child was born, I don't have a long history as a single woman, so I'll let single women themselves—including some never married, some divorced, and some widowed—provide insight into these touchy areas.

Encouraging my survey participants to be honest with those

of us who are married, I gave them the following sentence starters: I wish…, Please don't…, and Please remember…. Here's what they wrote:

- **I wish** married women would just listen and openly sympathize with me when I need it. No statements of "Oh, I'm sure you'll be married soon." That's very abrupt and assuming. It doesn't identify with my present pain.

- **I wish** they knew that I long to sit in church with a Christian husband and children. I wish they would realize how blessed they are. I wish they knew that it takes a lot of energy to keep going places alone or to find someone to do an activity with. It is easier to stay home than to be alone in a group of couples.

- **I wish** they knew that I don't feel incomplete without a husband.

- **I wish** they knew that I enjoy having "my own" checkbook and schedules.

- **I wish** they knew that I do appreciate my freedom.

- **I wish** there were more opportunities to be with women and men. It's more interesting to listen to men and women talk.

- **I wish** married women would understand a single woman's need to belong. We desire relationships with married women and couples, but it can be hard if conversation usually revolves around spouses or children.

- **I wish** married women would include widows for lunches, shopping, or just get-togethers. Because I am so involved with church-related activities, I'm sure many think I don't have time to be invited out.

- **Please *don't*** matchmake me with any single male just because he's breathing. Matchmaking is OK if you know both personalities and there is possible compatibility and you've prayed about it.

- **Please *don't*** say that I'll find someone....

- **Please *don't*** think I'm trying to "snag" your man. Trust me to have fun and laugh, whether with a man or woman.

- **Please *don't*** assume I have more time to volunteer for activities.

- **Please *don't*** assume I would initiate a relationship if I desired one.

- **Please remember** I have to make all my decisions alone.

- **Please remember** that I do appreciate your friendships and I do enjoy hearing about your children and lives.

- **Please remember** that even though there are two of you (or more) and I take care of only me, there's no one to share my load. Work and chores are done by one person.

- **Please remember** that I may not want to have married women "on the lookout" for a husband for me.

- **Please remember** that as a widow, I enjoy hearing a man express his viewpoint.

As I read through their responses, I also liked the way some women use humor to handle singleness issues. Viola, a friend of mine, says that during her first trip to London she wanted to take a cruise on the Thames River. She "queued up" in the "single" line (because of her marital status) only to discover "single" meant one way as opposed to round trip!

Born to Shop

Whether we're married or single, one common ground many of us share is our born-to-shop mentality. One day Missy heard her five-year-old son trying out his newly acquired art form known as the "joke" on his four-year-old sister. "Why did the chicken cross the road?" he asked.

"To get to the mall?" his sister replied.

I guess some of us discover the joys of shopping early. What is there about a bargain—or even the potential of a sale—that magnetically draws us to the malls, to the garage sales, even to the catalogs? And why does our definition of shopping differ so greatly from that of men?

I once heard author John Trent point out the differences between male and female shopping trips. It went something like this: A man goes to the discount store to buy one item. Generally, as if wearing blinders, he goes directly to the department that carries that item, takes his purchase to the checkout counter, and leaves with that one item. A woman, on the other hand, meanders through every department between the front door and the desired department, as if in a maze. Because of her relational nature she's *touching* other items all along her path.

I laughed as my mind instantly replayed many of my shopping trips. I have to touch the soft-looking bath towels, pick up a candle to smell it, rub my hand over a little velvet baby dress, and tap the nature-sounds-with-music CD display to sample its melodic offerings.

I'm not intimidated by Trent's comparison. I like it. I like being relational, whether it's to people or things. And I like the fact that I'm not *so* focused that I can't savor the sights, sounds, smells, textures, and even tastes of the things around me. Do you think grocery stores plop those free-sample ladies in the middle of the aisles to keep men from getting hungry while they shop? I don't think so. I think they're there to help women *relate* to the product—how delicious it smells, how great it tastes, how easy it is to prepare, complete with serving suggestions.

But I think there's another side to our magnetic pull toward the shopping experience—caretaking. We're always looking out for bargains and being mindful of things our families need.

A few weeks ago I was speaking for the second year in a row at a conference on the East Coast. The schedule allowed the speakers to spend a few hours at an outlet mall across from our hotel the morning after we arrived. Last year I found some terrific bargains on clothes in my hard-to-find size, so I eagerly awaited this opportunity. Unfortunately, the conference director had made reservations for us at a different motel miles from the mall and forgot to tell us.

Another of the speakers and I had packed few clothes, counting on our shopping excursion. And a third woman displayed the early symptoms of mall withdrawal! Sensing potential mutiny, the conference director let us borrow a van and we got our "shopping fix"!

My husband has often razzed me for my inability to "stay on task" in the store, but actually, I think my what-else-might-we-need-soon-as-long-as-I'm-here mindset is more efficient than the horse-with-blinders approach. But isn't it funny how a quick shopping trip can turn into a grueling all-day expedition—especially with little ones in tow?

Living near the Mall of America, the largest shopping mall in the United States, I delight in an occasional marathon at this grandiose monument to consumerism. On one such trip with my sister, we came upon a kiosk in the middle of the people traffic which displayed T-shirts with clever sayings. My sister couldn't resist the one that read: "I am woman! I am invincible! I am tired!" That's our world.

"I Enjoy Being a Girl"

We're women. We work hard. We have our "If onlys" but we also have resources, especially if we look to the God who created us this way to lead us into the full, rich lives He wants us to enjoy.

We all probably could list several things we hate, dislike, or merely tolerate about our womanhood, but when we think of our intricate design, it's absolutely astounding! I've been encouraged with how positive many women are about their gender. As the last question on my very long survey, I wrote, "After putting you through all this, I have to ask: What do you like most about being a woman?" Here are some of their comments:

- My femininity. I enjoy being soft when it's called for and strong when necessary.

- I like not being afraid of being sensitive. A lot of men are.

- Lots of perks! I've been stranded and helpless many times, and people are more likely to help a woman. I enjoy a woman's intuition, experiences, and fellowship.

- I like to be ornamental at times. I also like to be a tomboy and throw everyone off!

- I appreciate being able to wear makeup, dress up, visit with my friends, and have lots of "girl talks."

- I like to be a woman because I get nice long letters from women friends, and I don't think men write to each other like that.

- I like that I was designed to experience the thrill of bearing life (my children).

- It's a real compliment when men help me put on my coat or offer their arm on the icy parking lot.

- The only alternative is being a man and I wouldn't want that! I like the qualities God gave women—the gentleness, the voice range, the mothering skills, the homemaking skills. Hey, don't get me wrong … I do not dislike men. I just wouldn't like to be one!

Competing or Complementing?

Remember that old song from Irving Berlin's musical *Annie, Get Your Gun*—"Anything You Can Do" (I Can Do Better)? Having inherited a bit of a tomboy streak from my mother, I remember growing up trying to prove to guys that I was just as good as they were (or better) in the classroom, at sports, even at a belching contest or two. Yet as I've matured (kind of), I've learned the beauty of men and women complementing each other rather than competing—in our marriages, in our jobs, in every area of life. Someone has said that when two people agree on absolutely everything, one of them is not necessary.

In his book *Men Are from Mars, Women Are from Venus*, John Gray says, "Men mistakenly expect women to think, communicate, and react the way men do; women mistakenly expect men to feel, communicate, and respond the way women do. *We have forgotten that men and women are supposed to be different.* As a result, our relationships are filled with unnecessary friction and conflict" (emphasis mine).[2]

God did not make a mistake in creating two genders. When Adam was the only human being in the Garden of Eden, God said, "It is not good"(Genesis 2:18). But after He created Eve, "God saw all that he had made, and it was *very* good" (Genesis 1:31, emphasis mine). Considering a conflict through both a male and female "lens" can be like putting on a pair of 3-D glasses to make sense of otherwise incomprehensible scribbly pictures. As we appreciate each other's perspectives, solutions can jump out at us in beautiful three-dimensional clarity.

The apostle Paul said, "I have learned the secret of being content." Then in the next verse he says, "I can do everything through him who gives me strength" (Philippians 4:12-13).

The more content we are with our womanhood hat—with who God made us to be—the more poise we'll demonstrate in balancing the other hats that quickly appear....

Study Questions

Get-acquainted questions:

As women, most of us wear many hats. Discuss with each other what hats you wear. What qualities of womanhood that God has given you do you like most? What areas do you need God's help to appreciate?

1. Read Genesis 1:26-28. After our Creator brought all of heaven and earth into existence, He decorated the world with greenery and flowers, populating it with elephants and emus, lions and lizards, angel fish and aardvarks. Then He created "man." Look at the pronouns in the Genesis 1 passage. How do we know that *man* in Scripture is a generic term for both male and female human beings? In whose image, then, are we as women created?

2. If each of us is God's unique creation, what implications does that have for how you view yourself and your talents?

3. Read Genesis 1:4, 10, 12, 18, 21, and 25. What common phrase appears in all of these verses? Read Genesis 2:18. What did God say was not good? When did God say His creation was *very* good? (See vv. 27 and 31.) What qualities common to women do you think "complete" humanity?

4. Read Proverbs 31:10. The King James Version of the Bible uses the term *virtuous woman*. What synonyms can you find in other translations? What worth does God put on a woman with these characteristics?

5. Read Proverbs 31:30. What two qualities of womanhood named in this verse frequently appear in the cover blurbs of women's magazines? What does God say is worthy of praise in a woman? How would you recognize a woman with that quality? How do you cultivate it in yourself?

6. Read Philippians 4:12-13. Where do we learn the secret of being content with how our Creator made us?

Thought to ponder this week:

If God created male and female in His image to complement one another, in what ways can we cooperate more and compete less with our male counterparts?

TWO

Does That Wedding Veil Still Fit?

~

My Role as a Wife

I love being … a wife—a completer, helper.
—Joanie Garborg
Her hats include those of editor,
wife of a publisher, mother
of one teenager.

My veil is the *only* thing that still fits from my wedding day!

Such a wonderful creation! It was lovingly made by my mother from a pearl and iridescent sequined tiara she found on sale and several yards of white netting. I like to get my veil out every once in a while, again trying to plant those funny little combs in my hair just the right way so my tiara won't slip off as it did countless times on our wedding day.

After more than a quarter of a century of marriage, I sometimes look back and think, *I didn't have a clue what I was getting into!* Premarital classes weren't big then. Marriage was a do-it-yourself, learn-as-you-go kit. We didn't have personality-assessment tools, such as MMPIs or Meyers-Briggs—though I think we got a Briggs & Stratton something-or-other for a wedding gift.

Looking back, it doesn't take much to *become* a wife. It seems rather simple in hindsight (though I'm sure some single women would take issue at that). But once you've found that special person, or he's found you, a simple "I do" or "I will" seals the matter. In two seconds, whether you are prepared for it or not, you *are* a wife. And suddenly every ounce of selfishness within your personality pops out all over. (At least that's how it was for me.)

Football!

Thanks to my mother and my healthy tomboy tendencies, I grew up loving baseball and following the St. Louis Cardinals (my hometown team) with great enthusiasm. I played field hockey in high school, learned archery and swimming at summer camp, and played softball, tennis, Ping-Pong, and other sports. But football never made sense to me. I went to a few games during high school, but I must admit the social aspects drew me there more than any understanding or enjoyment of the game.

So, as Murphy's Law would have it, I married an ardent football fan.

Sunday after Sunday, I fussed as Steve sat transfixed before the television for not one but two three-hour stints of pro football. Saturday after Saturday, I fumed while he watched as many college games as the networks could squeeze into their schedules.

During each interminably long game, of course, the television, not I, was the focus of attention. We were newlyweds. I deserved a little attention, didn't I? But if I talked to my husband I felt like an intruder. And he seldom *initiated* any conversation during a game.

To add insult to injury, one day I asked him which team he was rooting for. "I don't really care who wins in this game," he said. "I just like to watch."

Can you imagine? What's the point?

For the life of me, I couldn't figure out the attraction in this silly game, with men in tight pants to make them look skinny on the bottom and shoulder pads to make them look huge on top. Furthermore, if they really wanted to get that ball from one end of the field to the other, why didn't they make the ball round, as in every other respectable sport?

The terminology also boggled my mind. My new husband tried to explain the four-downs-to-get-a-first-down concept, but I've never been good at math—and this certainly didn't help. Then the system of scoring—sometimes six points, sometimes three, sometimes two, sometimes one—made about as much sense to me as Einstein's theory of relativity, whatever that is.

It's hard for me to admit how long I made sure Steve knew I resented his devotion to the sport. But I know my attitude worsened when the networks aided and abetted the American male addiction by adding *Monday Night Football* and an occasional Thursday night game. Never can get enough of that hit-'em-hard, ring-their-bell, whatever-it-takes-to-get-that-ball-over-the-line contest so we can say we're number one (until next week), right?

I sided with the person who characterized the stadium experience of football as fifty thousand people desperately in need of exercise watching twenty-two men desperately in need of rest.

The Day I Knew I Married the Wrong Man

It wasn't just football. Steve and I are proof positive that opposites attract. He likes a quiet evening at home. I invent excuses to get out of the house. He weighs all decisions and actions carefully. I'm spontaneous and impulsive. He measures his words. I think about what I say *after* I've said it.

John Gray's book title *Men Are from Mars, Women Are from Venus* describes us perfectly. Some days it's like we're from two different galaxies, much less planets.

When I first met Steve, I was convinced he was a stick-in-the-mud. He didn't seem like any fun. But over a period of months, I fell in love with him—his steadiness, his calm and quiet manner, his dry wit, and *his* unbelievable love for *me*.

After we were married, my unrealistic expectations of everlasting spine-tingling romance, my focus on my own needs, and my disillusionment with how much work it took to keep a marriage and a household together grew. Then the children came along, and I stewed about how seldom Steve helped around the house.

Don't get me wrong. Life wasn't always miserable. From time to time Steve would surprise me with a weekend getaway, or I would actually tell him when something was bothering me instead of expecting him to read my mind. We've had some great times together, but too often my discontent flailed its ugly tentacles.

Some days I was sure I had married the wrong man. This wasn't the way happily-ever-after love was supposed to be. More often than I'd like to admit, I didn't *feel* very loving toward Steve. I even wondered if I had fallen out of love.

But one day I woke up to the reality that my husband's

personality wasn't going to change. I knew I couldn't change my personality either. But if I didn't want to be miserable for the rest of my life, I'd better change my attitude about the differences between us.

Ending the marriage was never an option. I had vowed before God—a very serious thing—and a church full of friends and relatives that we would remain married to one another until *death*. And since murder wasn't an option either, I started to take a long, hard look at the situation.

If I couldn't change my husband, what could I change about me?

Over a period of time, little by little, I realized that my wanting more of his attention during football games was nothing short of selfishness. My desire for breathtaking, endless romance was not only unrealistic (fueled by fantasies on the silver screen and my little nineteen-incher at home), but such fantasies could also lead to exhaustion. And my expectations that he should know what I needed without my telling him smacked of mind-reading nonsense.

I'm glad our wedding vows required us to say, "I will," rather than "I do." Every disagreement about how money should be spent or whose parents to spend holidays with or how to discipline the kids has called for a conscious decision of the will. Because of our commitment on our wedding day to live together harmoniously as husband and wife, we daily need to commit to making this marriage work. We won't give up. There's too much at stake.

For me the give-and-take of marriage has meant learning how four downs can make a first down and honestly caring about my husband's enjoyment of the game. I found out he *would* pay attention to me if I showed an interest in what he was interested in. And now, when I watch football with him, I can even tell where the ball is most of the time.

I'm still learning how to communicate my feelings and needs and trying to remember to thank him when he helps around the house. Funny how much more frequently he helps when I let him know I *need* his help!

Love Is Something You Do

Love is an action verb. During those times when I didn't *feel loving* toward Steve, I could still consciously *do* something nice for him, such as making sure we got home in time to see his Green Bay Packers or making his favorite dinner or doing a chore I knew he hated. Instead of always waiting for him to be romantic, I began looking for opportunities to tell him I loved him (both by verbal expressions and in love notes on the napkin in his lunch bag and other strategic places).

Feelings followed actions. The more I *did* for him and tried to build him up, the more my *love* for him grew.

One weekend I even kidnapped him to make sure we **had** time to nurture our love relationship. At that time, my husband and I were cleaning a couple's house every week in exchange for piano lessons for our three kids. So before Steve arrived home from work that long-awaited day, I packed a suitcase for two and stowed it in the back of our station wagon. Thanks to a two-for-one coupon book, I arranged for dinner and motel reservations for one night, then hired a baby sitter, and gave her a key so she could be waiting for us when we returned home in our grubbies from our piano lesson and cleaning jaunt.

The baby sitter parked out of sight, and when we drove into our driveway, the kids (who had kept the secret well) ran into the house with the baby sitter. I told Steve to move over into the passenger seat because I was taking him for a little drive. I then handed him a blindfold, which—much to my amazement—he put on with only mild protestations and embarrassment, probably because it was dark outside. I did let him take the blindfold off when we reached the motel. I should have realized my engineer husband would figure out about where we were anyway by the duration of our ride and the direction of each turn.

I had picked up the room key earlier, so we were able to go directly to our room, get cleaned up for an elegant dinner, and enjoy a glorious evening away—just as our middle child often advised: "Now you two go out and pretend you don't have any kids!"

The Upside of the Downside

I'd still rather watch baseball than football. And I'll admit that the background noise of a televised football game facilitates my Sunday afternoon naps with Pavlovian predictability. But I have even been known to watch football when my husband wasn't around.

A little humor helps as well. One Saturday Steve was watching his second college game of the day, and I knew he planned to watch the high school prep bowl championship game that evening. I was busy in another room, but I went in and checked his pulse and other vital signs to make sure he wasn't "OD-ing" on football that day.

It's a good thing I learned the game, though. The football-loving gene manifested itself with greater intensity in our son's DNA, creating a wonderful bond between the two males in our household—a bond that could have fueled my bitterness if I hadn't dealt with it. And our son now makes his living as a sports and news broadcaster!

Over the course of our marriage Steve has made many concessions to accommodate my interests as well. When our kids were little, every Sunday he had to try to corral our three rambunctious youngsters after Sunday school while they waited for me to finish singing with the choir for our church's second service. (No wonder he vegged out during Sunday afternoon football games.) He also has come to enjoy camping in spite of the inordinate amount of work it takes just to pull out of the driveway. And he has sacrificed many of his own needs and desires to help me meet writing deadlines, get ready for company, or leave town for a convention or speaking engagement.

The longer I'm married, the more I realize I definitely married the *right* man for me. I am so grateful God knew exactly what I needed. Steve patiently waits in the craft aisle while I try to find twelve skeins of yarn with the same dye lot number for a new afghan pattern, he provides a wise sounding board for speaking and writing projects, and his English skills make him an excellent final proofreader of everything I write. I shudder when I think of some of the guys I dated who wouldn't know a participle from a parsnip!

His calm, steady, logical characteristics, which, at times, can raise my blood pressure, have often rescued me from some impulse-driven catastrophe. And his sense of direction has at least steered me in the right direction to start with—though if there's any possible way to get lost, I'll usually find it. My sister once told her daughter-in-law, "You know how if you turn most people around three times, they lose their sense of direction? With Joyce, you don't have to turn her around."

Sometimes we get so wrapped up in our differences and problems that we don't step back and appreciate the good things we have. We forget the wonderful qualities that drew us to our husbands in the first place.

During the premarital counseling of every couple our pastor marries, he asks the prospective bride what qualities in her husband-to-be drew her to love him and vice versa. They each write down these qualities, and the pastor reads them to the couple during their wedding ceremony. Since many weddings are videotaped, I think this is a great idea. Sometimes we might need to remind ourselves why we ever loved this guy in the first place. Maybe we should all make such a list and frame it so we never forget!

Most of us can find the upside of the downside—if we work at it.

Design: Better Than a Paris Original

When the downside looms too large, we need help, and God is bigger than the downside. Our wifely hat, a designer original, came from the greatest creative mind of all time—our Creator's. Marriage was His idea in the beginning, so I go to Him when I need help.

I'm always amazed that some people still refer to wives as "helpmeets" or "helpmates." That was never a biblical term. The King James Bible says that God watched Adam in that new Garden He had made, and when God looked around at all the animals, He said, "It is not good that the man should be alone; I will make him an help meet for him" (Genesis 2:18). The old English word *meet* means suitable, as it is rendered in some of the newer translations.

So God designed Eve—the first wife who ever lived—to become the only suitable helper for this man whom God knew needed someone special to make his life complete. And He used a little piece of Adam—his rib—to design this new creature.

Let's face it. Adam had a veritable zoo around him, but it wasn't enough to make his life whole. All the adages about a dog being man's best friend are nonsense! That's *our* privilege.

Just as Eve always knew one of her ribs came from Adam, you and I, from the time God joins us together with our husbands, will always carry a little bit of that man around inside us.

Our role, as wives, is to complement or help round out our husbands' lives. They need us even when they don't acknowledge it. Sometimes they'd like to acknowledge it, but they don't know how. What an awesome responsibility God designed for us in this role!

Variations in Style

Just as a designer wedding veil might come in white or ecru, long or short, pearls or sequins, marriages come in varying styles, too.

The blueprints for matters such as who does the cooking, who cleans the toilets, and who tries to keep our heads above water financially are best jointly decided by husband and wife according to each spouse's strengths—or weaknesses. For instance, after Steve *tried* to help me balance my checkbook when we were engaged, by mutual agreement he has taken care of all the financial arrangements since our wedding.

Cooking is my domain. During a miscarriage I had within the first year of our marriage, the doctor sent me home to bed and told Steve to cook me a light dinner, such as baked chicken and mashed potatoes. To this day I tease him about the chicken jerky and wallpaper paste we ate that night.

On the other hand, my married daughter and her husband share cooking responsibilities because they both enjoy it, both have talents in that area, and both tease each other about their cooking disasters.

Sometimes problems arise when we expect our marriage to follow the same style as that of our parents. First, we each have different models in our families. And second, our husbands may or may not be like our fathers.

My dad loved to

    a. fix things

    b. build things

    c. remodel things

    d. do all of the above.

Steve loves to

    e. do none of the above.

After all these years, I still get frustrated with that. Steve has tackled some projects here and there, but "handyman" will never be on the top-ten list of titles he covets.

The main thing for us to remember about style in our role as wives is that the home we establish when we get married is to be a refuge—a safe place—away from all the craziness in our world. When we talk about building a home together, we're talking about building each other up, not tearing each other down. The Bible says that the excellent wife "brings [her husband] good, not harm, all the days of her life" (**Proverbs** 31:12). And he, in turn, "has full confidence in her" (v. 11).

Practicing a Stylish Presence

That kind of mutual respect and caring for one another leaves no room for selfishness. So, at the risk of oversimplification, let me suggest two keys for strengthening our marriages:

1. Get rid of selfishness.

2. Get full of commitment.

That may *sound* like oversimplification, but, in reality, I think a lot of our wedded "unbliss" could disappear if we truly worked on those two areas.

Husband bashing is so common today that it's easy to fall into that rut. But it's difficult to engage in husband bashing and build our husbands up at the same time.

The U.S. Army slogan says, "Be all that you can be in the army." But the designer of husband-wife relationships says marriage is the place where, by building each other up in the good times and the tough times, we can truly be all we were meant to be.

We need to thank God for our marriage, nurture it, revel in it, and enhance it. With God's help, we can commit ourselves to making it work. A strong marriage is the best gift we can give to our children and to the world at large. After all, we never know who's watching us, looking for hope in their own marriage. So hang in there. It's worth it....

Study Questions

1. Read Genesis 2:18. When God created Eve, He said He was making a helper suitable to Adam. If you're married, in what ways do you think God chose you for your husband because you were "suitable"? If you're not married, what have you observed about the "suitability" of couples you know?

2. What possible things can warp a couple's view of their God-given suitability? What can we do about the areas in which we don't feel well suited? If you're married, sometime this week ask your husband how you're doing on meeting his needs and being a suitable helper for him. In what ways do you feel you make your husband whole?

3. Read Genesis 2:20-24. Which bone of Adam's did God use in creating Eve? What possible symbolism can you see in that?

4. Read Proverbs 18:22. What is God's opinion of the role of a wife? According to this verse, what can a wife bring her husband? In what ways do you think you can do that?

5. Read Proverbs 19:13-14. What good and bad qualities of some wives does God point out in these verses? What are

some practical ways we can avoid the bad quality and nurture the good one?

6. Read Ephesians 5:21-33. God tells us to submit to one another, but He particularly reemphasizes that wives should be submissive. How is this significant, especially in our generation? The passage also specifically reminds husbands to love their wives. What significance do you see in that—especially in our generation? Does that passage say we are only to be submissive if our husbands are loving toward us?

7. Read Proverbs 31:11-12. According to this passage, what gives a husband confidence in his wife?

THREE

Has Anyone Seen My Chauffeur's Cap?

~

My Role as a Mother, Need-Meeter, Nurturer, et al.

I like feeling a little hand in mine, knowing that the child it belongs to is depending on me to lead him or her the right way.
—Marjorie Havens
Her hats include those of children's Bible teacher and craft leader, wife of heavy equipment operator, mother of five grown children, grandmother of eleven.

Here's where things get a bit more hectic.

Becoming a mother is quite a bit more *painful* than becoming a wife—usually. We women all know why God chose the fairer sex, rather than macho men, to bear children. If men had to suffer through ankles the size of grapefruits, a jumbo-jet belly that defies any sense of equilibrium, and fourteen to thirty-six hours of crying for deliverance or a quick trip to heaven, we all know that every child born into this world would be an only child. "Never again!" we can hear them screaming now!

One young father-to-be accompanied his wife on her first visit to the OB/Gyn's office to find out if the over-the-counter early pregnancy test was as reliable as commercials say. Seeing the stirrups protruding from the end of the examining table like menacing robot arms, he nearly bolted from the room.

Women, on the other hand, often become ecstatic about their impending role. Mother-to-be Missy was so excited when she got the stroller she wanted that she couldn't wait until the baby was born to try it out. Covering a large, plump teddy bear with lots of blankets in the stroller, she and her husband wheeled their precious stuffed cargo around their favorite mall all afternoon.

Mission Impossible?

Motherhood, however, is another role we're never quite ready for. Despite the numerous freebie magazines in the obstetrician's office, mothering is still a some-assembly-required project. So many questions you never thought to ask. So much nobody prepared you for:

- How fast do you have to get that diaper on, anyway (especially with a man-child!)?

- Which of all these noises our baby makes are normal and which ones require a panic call to the doctor?

- Why didn't somebody tell me that monitoring and cleaning up after bodily functions would consume 93 percent of my time?

And going beyond the physical and emotional needs of our children, bringing them up in "the nurture and admonition of the Lord" (Ephesians 6:4, KJV) in our upside-down, black-is-white, bad-means-good world seems like *Mission Impossible* personified.

Sometimes Scripture makes it sound so simple. King Solomon glibly wrote that the virtuous woman's children "rise up and call her blessed" (Proverbs 31:28, KJV). I don't know about yours, but mine would habitually rise up and start fighting before I was even awake.

Bible stories aren't very specific in the how-to department either. Jochabed (Moses' mother), Hannah (Samuel's mother), and Eunice (Timothy's mother) never seemed to have any problems with their kids. They just taught them the Scriptures, and the kids gobbled it up, it seems.

Some days, sheer survival seemed an ambitious goal for me—never mind imparting spiritual truth!

And have you ever noticed what quick-change artists we have become with our many hats as mothers? There have been times when I have had to change hats so fast—from housemaid to nurse to hostess to seamstress to chef to chauffeur to tutor to entertainer to cheerleader—that I got dizzy!

Lest anyone consider the title of this book a gross exaggeration (it's called *hyperbole* in literary terms—exaggeration for effect), one day I actually sat down and listed every hat I currently wear or have worn in my lifetime. Without much thinking and in a short period of time, I listed 150 hats!

I quit counting out of exhaustion.

Admittedly some roles overlap, but each requires an investment of time—some small, some significant. And with the role of motherhood comes a plethora (I do so love that word!) of other hats.

Heresy in Counted Cross-Stitch

One day I noticed a framed, counted cross-stitch project in the window of a craft shop. A sad-faced little boy looked up beseechingly at his mom while the stitchery spelled out the message: God couldn't be everywhere; that's why He created mothers.

Oh, isn't that cute, I thought, ducking into the store to check the kit's price tag. *Hey, wait a minute,* I corrected myself. *That's heresy!*

I doubt that the kit's designer deliberately contradicted good theology. I'm sure he or she wanted to help mothers feel the importance of their tasks. But the Bible clearly teaches that God not only *can* be everywhere—He *is* everywhere!

"'Can anyone hide in secret places so that I cannot see him?' declares the Lord. 'Do not I fill heaven and earth?'" (Jeremiah 23:24) "For the Lord your God will be with you wherever you go" (Joshua 1:9).

Theologians call that *omnipresence.* I call it comforting!

Children have a way of wandering out of the yard, of leaving us to go to that great intimidating place called school (where we have little control over what happens), of attending parties (given by people we may not know well), and of not coming home when they're supposed to.

I remember the night our six-year-old daughter got lost among the tens of thousands of people at the state fair. Only after an interminable, heart-racing search did we find her by the "haunted house." I still shudder when I think about it. We hear so many news reports of unspeakable things done to kidnapped children! It's hard not to be fearful. And our concern doesn't end when they flit away from the nest.

So I've decided to reverse that craft-store motto: No matter how careful we try to be, "Mothers can't be everywhere. That's why they need God." Maybe someone should design a cross-stitch pattern of that!

Throughout all the stages of our children's lives we need to ask the Lord to embroider on our hearts and minds His ever-present care—both for our children and for us. Kids can be loud. Demanding. Unappreciative. Messy. Calamity catalysts. Yet they can also be hilarious. Loving. Warm. Snuggly. Heart melters.

Take My Hand

Amid tragedies and comedies, each stage of motherhood brings new challenges. And each new challenge brings new opportunities to develop our prayer muscles and strengthen our bond with the Lord.

- While an infant, our first child has a high fever in the middle of the night. As I walk the floor with him, he writhes in my arms, *screaming incessantly*, not understanding why he is so miserable. My husband and I *worry incessantly*, not understanding why the doctor isn't returning our panic call. Challenge!

- A mother finds her toddler feeding oatmeal to the VCR. Challenge!

- While playing outdoors our preschooler and her big sister race to our front door. Reaching the porch, the little one puts her arms out to stop herself and crashes through the glass storm door, nearly severing an artery. Blood everywhere! Challenge!

- Our middle child comes home from grade school one day, crying because the yuppie kids teased her about her clothes. The girl sitting behind her had reached into our daughter's collar to examine the label and delivered the ultimate insult: "Where'd your mom get this? At Target— on sale?" Challenge!

- A high-schooler forgets it's band day and leaves his instrument at home. "I know they need to learn to be responsible," the mom says, "but I find it extremely hard not to run it to school for them." Challenge!

- A college student comes home in tears because her boyfriend or "un-boyfriend" (depending on when you ask) of the past four years has just informed her he spent most of the previous weekend with her best friend. Challenge!

- At forty-four, in my fifth year of grueling studies toward a bachelor's degree, I listen as our oldest daughter and her fiancé tell us they want to get married two-and-a-half months after I graduate. Three of us in the family are already amassing school loans at the time. Challenge!

Many of the women who responded to my survey in preparation for this book mentioned how vital it was for them to know that God was there no matter what they were going through! I couldn't agree more!

When I was about six, we visited my uncle's church, and he asked me to sing a solo. I complied, singing "Precious Lord, Take My Hand." I wonder now what I, as a first grader, knew about being tired, weak, and worn. But I've certainly known those feelings since I became a mother!

There have been times when all I could do was envision myself literally placing my hand in the Lord's hand and asking

Him to take over. Other times, in bouts of depression or grief or disappointment, I knew I didn't even have the strength to lift my hand for Him to hold. I needed Him to *take* my hand before He could lead me on.

Ever-Present, Ever-Faithful

Remembering that God is with us provides perspective in the midst of all these mothering challenges.

He is here—more powerful than a two-year-old's temper tantrum, able to solve great problems after a single prayer, faster than a speeding meteor to show us His unfailing love when ours has run completely dry. Because He holds our hand and leads us on, we have *"strength for today* and bright hope for tomorrow," as the old hymn says. If I've learned anything from mothering, it's to ask for God's strength and wisdom one day, one moment, at a time.

- Strength while wearing my cleaning whiz hat, trying to comb milk-squishy Cheerios out of shag carpeting.

- Wisdom in wearing my problem solver hat, trying to figure out how to help a middle-schooler catch up from a multi-week homework-procrastination binge.

- Strength while wearing my court jester hat, trying to cure a child's hypochondria with a generous dose of humor.

- Wisdom while wearing my referee hat in a crossfire of "I did nots" and "You did toos."

The Lord also gives us *hope for tomorrow*. That's what faith is—"the evidence of things we cannot yet see" (Hebrews 11:1, NLT). As our children grow bigger, so do their problems—

physical, emotional, and spiritual. And when they meet a genuine catastrophe head-on, we, as mothers, carry their heavy hearts as our own.

Mary King, a North Carolina mom, struggled with her emotions as her grown daughter Nancy needed kidney transplant surgery and Nancy's older sister Debbie proved a suitable donor. One day Mary was mulling over Genesis 22—God asking Abraham to sacrifice his son, Isaac. She wondered what Abraham must have felt as he traveled up that mountain, knowing what lay ahead for his son.

"I could relate," she says, "thinking about my two daughters—one willing to make a tremendous sacrifice for her sister in order to save her life." As the time drew closer for the surgery, Mary's heart began to ache for both daughters. "My love for my oldest said, 'There must be another way.' My love for my youngest said, 'There is no other way. Thank you, Debbie, for being willing.'"

Mary felt grateful for the little peek into God's emotions as He sent His Son to become a sacrifice. "In Psalm 22 He opens His heart to us," Mary says, "and we come to appreciate even more the great sacrifice."

Motherhood's hat, by definition, is studded with struggles, hassles, and tensions. Juggling all our responsibilities often leaves us with emotional vertigo. But there's nothing like having children of our own to help us appreciate our dear heavenly Father, who cares so much for us. Because our ever-present, ever-faithful, ever-loving God is with us at all times, we can talk with Him about every situation—good or bad—while we're going through it.

He can handle our questions: Lord, we've given our children to you, but when are you going to whip this kid into shape?

He can handle our doubts: Lord, why must our baby's life hang in the balance like this? You're all-powerful. Can't you fix it?

He can handle our fears: Lord, it's 3:20 A.M., and our daughter got off work more than three hours ago! Please protect her wherever she is and bring her home soon!

Our all-wise, Almighty God deserves our trust.

A Privileged Role Model

I've been so impressed with Jesus' mother as a role model for mothering. I suspect she didn't always do everything right, but her heart was right. I think it all dates back to that day the angel told her not to be afraid; God had chosen her for a unique task. What an awesome responsibility—to carry within her the Son of God, to raise the Savior of the world!

As I see it, in accepting that overwhelming responsibility and privilege, Mary modeled three character traits: confidence, trust, and reflection.

Confidence, Not Fear

The angel told Mary, "The Lord is with you" (Luke 1:28), so, "Do not be afraid" (v. 30).

One day a friend at church told me that because of all the evil in the world around us, she had been fearful about her parenting role. But then she realized that God has chosen each of us mothers in this particular time frame to parent these particular children for Him.

Isn't that an exciting thought? He has entrusted these children to our care right now. He could have put us in "the olden days" when we think things were so much easier. (Oh, really?) But He chose *us*—for *these* kids! Right now! And He always equips us beforehand for anything He asks us to do.

One day at lunch one of my coworkers made a powerful statement with a single word. We were talking about the challenges of teenagers, and she simply said her son's name and rolled her eyes! It was the perfect time to pass along my friend's observation: "But just think, the Lord entrusted that child to you, my friend. And God doesn't make any mistakes."

These are good thoughts to remember as you're going into the delivery room—or coming out of the principal's office. "Do not be afraid. The Lord is with you." Put your hand in His hand and don't be afraid of what's ahead. He knows what lies before you, He is in control, and He can handle it all.

Brenda, a mother of four in her thirties, says it was only her belief that God is in control that got her through the most severe test of her life. When her third son, Abel, was a year and a half old, he began having severe seizures—sometimes six to eight times a minute! About a year passed before doctors diagnosed Angelman's Syndrome—a rare genetic disorder—and found two medications to help him. Severely retarded, Abel will never talk, Brenda says, "but he is a joy in our lives.

"Even though this was a real time of testing," she continues, "we never doubted that God was in control. He has been so faithful to take us through the difficult times. Without my faith I know I would have fallen apart as all our hopes and dreams for this baby did."

Whether it's medical crises or the daily concerns of whether we're "doing it right," as mothers, our natural tendency is to fear. But "God did not give us a spirit of timidity—of cowardice," says 2 Timothy 1:7. "[He has given us a spirit] of

power and of love and of calm and well-balanced mind"
(AMPLIFIED).

Trust, Not Worry

Mary wondered how God was going to pull off this miraculous conception. I can almost hear her thoughts: *A baby without a human father? That's not how my mom explained the birds and the bees.* But Mary chose to trust God instead of worrying about how He was going to work it all out.

The angel had said, "Nothing is impossible with God."

Mary responded, "I am the Lord's servant.... May it be to me as you have said" (Luke 1:37-38).

Raising the child who became the Savior of the world was a huge responsibility. Raising *any* child is a daunting responsibility. And trying to raise more than one child while meeting our husband's needs and wearing all our other womanly hats challenges even the most organized among us. That's why we need a constant trust in the Lord and the wisdom of His Word.

Of course the older our children grow, the less control we have and the more we have to depend on God to exercise control. Our natural tendency is to worry. But remember: Moms can't be everywhere. That's why we need God.

My Aunt Claire remembers the most worrisome night of her life back in the 1950s. Once a week her husband, Larry, and a man named Stuart Wilson conducted a children's Bible club in a low-income section of their city, usually returning home about 9:30 or 10:00 P.M. Claire's five small children, close in age, kept her busy throughout the evening, so she didn't think much about Larry's return until the clock struck 11:00. Then 12:00. He still hadn't arrived.

With a telephone strike crippling communication, Claire had to dial an operator to get special permission to make a call. Though the operator suggested Claire call the hospitals and hinted Larry might have just stopped off at a bar somewhere (she obviously didn't know him), Claire got permission to call Mr. Wilson.

"I don't understand why he isn't home yet," Mr. Wilson told her. "Larry was going home when I left him at eight o'clock." He promised to call her again in half an hour. If Larry hadn't returned, Mr. Wilson promised to retrace the route in case of car trouble or other difficulties. "But don't worry," Mr. Wilson said. "If anything serious had happened, the police would have come to tell you about it."

Claire tried to busy herself, got ready for bed, and made sure the children were OK. But she did worry. Though generally a calm person, she began pacing the floor. Panic built within her as the minutes ticked on. She thought of all the things that could have happened.

She went outside to see if Larry was coming, but instead she saw a police car coming up the hill, shining a light on all the house numbers. "I felt like ice inside," she says. She went inside and donned her robe to meet the officer at the door. But when she returned, he had already gone past.

"It was such an awful experience for me," she says. She got down on her knees and laid her head on the sofa. "Lord, I don't know where Larry is or what's happened to him," she prayed with tears rolling down her face. "But I know he's in your hands, and I never—ever—in my whole life want to feel this kind of worry again." Her heart settled into a comfortable peace.

Mr. Wilson arrived a little later, and he sat and talked

with Claire until about 1:30, when they heard Larry come in through the downstairs garage door. Mr. Wilson went to meet him, and Larry came upstairs bewildered. "Don't you remember when I left I told you I might be a little late?" (One-thirty is a little late?) "I went back to work to finish up some projects I hadn't gotten done today."

Claire recalls, "There was no real problem there. It was all conceived in my mind. But the Lord gave me peace even before I knew Larry was OK. There have been lots of times I could have worried with all the things the children were doing—sports, fishing, boating, diving off cliffs, and so forth, but I never felt that kind of worry again."

In my own early child-rearing years I've experienced a miscarriage, nearly losing our son at birth, suffering with our second child through the doctors' continuous bafflement and finally surgery for a painful wrist condition, and a scary night in the hospital after our third child—as a toddler—ingested my mom's heart medication and Valium. And those are just the *physical* traumas. As they've grown bigger, so have the concerns at times. Claiming God's promise that He is always with me (see Isaiah 41:10) has turned many a night of worry into a lifetime of trusting Him because I know He is always in control.

We, like Jesus' mother, need to remember who it is who is telling us He's got everything under control. And as we remember the ways He's helped us through tough times before, we can more easily trust Him again.

Reflection, Not Distraction

After Mary gave birth to Jesus in that smelly, disgusting stable, remember how the shepherds came and told their remarkable story about the angels' appearance to them? They bowed in front of the baby and worshiped Him. I can hardly imagine what that would have been like. "But Mary treasured up all these things and pondered them in her heart" (Luke 2:19). The shepherds' visit confirmed again her amazing privilege and responsibility.

I'm not sure I would have responded so positively. Cattle and sheep and donkeys breathing down my neck while I gave birth, and a straw "mattress"—without even a mattress cover—to place my baby on? I think a shard of doubt may have cut through my mind: "God, are You sure this is the birthing room You had in mind for the Savior of the world?"

Our natural tendency is to be distracted by all that's going on both inside and outside our homes, but God wants us to treasure the precious and fleeting moments with our youngsters—big or little—and to reflect on all they can teach us about our heavenly Father.

When asked what they would do differently as a mom if they could start over, some women said they would have more children. Others said they would have fewer. But most said, in various ways, they would spend more time with their kids one on one and enjoy each stage of their growing-up years more.

One mom said, "I would show more love to my children individually, especially the youngest, who came along when I was so busy I guess I didn't let him know he was important. I thought we had good times together, but his adult life is so messed up with depression that he thinks everyone would be better off if he had never been born."

Another said she would pray for her children more. "I did pray for them, but as I grow older," she says, "I know prayer for those we love is the greatest gift we can ever give them."

A third said, "I would enjoy to the hilt every second of the day while the children are growing up and not be soooo busy!"

Cherishing the times we have with our kids strengthens our bonds and stores up happy memories to soften our empty nest someday. But treasuring our times with "our young" is far different than letting our kids "rule the roost."

Where's the Center?

Somehow, within a generation or two, some families have gone from "Children should be seen and not heard," to "Eye hath not seen nor ear heard what we'll sacrifice to make sure our kids have everything!"

I know what it's like to want your kids to have more than you had growing up, and I admit we went overboard sometimes. But I'm concerned about parents who are knocking themselves out to make sure their kids have *all* the "in" toys. I ache for parents who chauffeur their kids to music lessons, gymnastics, karate, and Little League—and that's just Monday's schedule!

A Christ-centered home, rather than a child-centered home, encourages the gifts and talents in each child—because God is the giver of all gifts—but keeps everyone's eyes on Christ and His kingdom to maintain balance in all the activities. We can't live our lives over through our kids. We also can't substitute taking them to countless activities for genuine one-on-one nurturing and faith building.

During a getaway weekend with my husband several months ago, we wondered why young children and parents were wandering around outside the motel. The preschoolers strutted around uncomfortably yet proudly in ruffly pink dresses or miniature suits complete with power ties. (By contrast, many of the parents looked like they had just made a desert crossing in a pickup truck.) We soon learned that the motel was hosting a "Cute Kid" contest, complete with trophies.

I wonder what we're teaching our children with Cute Kid contests and frenetic schedules of endless activities in which we expect them to excel. Extracurricular activities *can* build character and people skills—just so we keep externals in perspective and remember that "God looks at the heart" (1 Samuel 16:7).

Do we have enough time in our scheduled rush to get to know our kids' hearts?

In Place of a Detailed Instruction Manual ...

So why didn't God give us a detailed instruction manual with thus-sayeth-the-Lord answers for every conceivable parenting situation? Why do publishers today crank out a never-ending stream of self-help books on parenting? Because parenting isn't a mechanical process.

The hat of motherhood (and fatherhood, for that matter) doesn't come in "one-size-fits-all" simplicity. Every parent and every child is a complex combination of DNA structure, personality quirks, endearing qualities, mood swings, and maddening tendencies. That's why Scripture doesn't include a book called *First Chronicles of Motherhood* or *The Encyclopedic Dictionary of Parenting Situations, Vol. 2.*

Better than that, the Lord gives us timeless, overall principles for pleasing Him and allows us the joy of discovering how to love and nurture our children as He loves and nurtures us. A mother who commits herself to pleasing God and seeks guidance from Him will find at her disposal the wisdom to deal with the "I did nots" and "You did toos." And if we're wise, we'll follow God's plan for developing relationships in which we can learn from each other rather than trying to prove we can make it on our own.

One mother who has adult children made this comment: "I've never stopped to really analyze my life and womanhood and motherhood. I've just enjoyed it!" What a great attitude!

Of course juggling outside employment with the full-time job of mothering complicates matters even more....

Study Questions

1. Read Proverbs 31:28. Look up the word *blessed* in a dictionary. Which of the definitions would fit here? Most of us will never hear our children rise to their feet at a mother-of-the-year banquet and call us "blessed." But if you have children, in what ways do you think they appreciate (or have appreciated) your role in their lives—even if they haven't expressed it? What qualities do you admire most in the mothers you know?

2. Read Jeremiah 23:24 and Joshua 1:9. In what ways can these verses be particularly encouraging to mothers? When are moms most afraid for their children?

3. Read Psalm 138:3 (in the King James Version, if possible). When all the tasks of motherhood seem overwhelming, where can mothers find strength for each day? If you have experienced a particularly good illustration of this type of help, tell the others in your group about it.

4. Read Luke 1:26-30 and Isaiah 41:10. In what ways is Jesus' mother, Mary, a good role model for us in faith? How can knowing God build confidence amid our many responsibilities?

5. Read 2 Timothy 1:7. There are many things in our world that can make a mom constantly fearful for her kids' safety and welfare, but how can we apply this verse to parenting?

6. Read Luke 1:45 (in the King James Version of the Bible, if possible). Luke 1 and 2 show that God could handle all Mary's questions, doubts, and fears. Knowing that, what is the special blessing promised here to women? In what ways can this promise build a mother's confidence?

7. Read Luke 2:19. What are some ways a mother can treasure, ponder, and enjoy each stage her children are in and remember the things God is teaching her?

FOUR

Why Didn't They Tell Me Hard Hats Must Be Worn in This Area?

~

*My Role as a Working Woman
(at Home or Abroad)*

*Man may work from sun to sun, but a woman's
work is never done.*

—An old proverb

My dear friend Linda, a petite blond farm girl from Iowa with a nursing degree, moved to Minneapolis to begin working at the veterans hospital. Nervous about her first day on the job and overwhelmed with big-city freeway traffic, she felt her stomach churning as she approached the hospital. Linda meandered around the parking lot, trying to find her assigned entrance. Not seeing the concrete parking-space curb just ahead, she slammed into it. Her head jerked forward, and she cracked her nose on the steering wheel.

In great pain and bleeding profusely, she stumbled inside, blood spurting all over her new white uniform, shoes, and nylons.

A couple of doctors inside the door gawked at this patient in a nurse's uniform. "Can we help you?" one of them asked.

"I think I need a doctor," Linda said in tears.

They quickly ushered her to the emergency room, where she introduced herself. "I'm the new coronary care nurse," she cried, cupping her hand over her face. "And I'm supposed to start work at seven, but I kind of hit my nose."

The top ear-nose-and-throat surgeon himself performed surgery on her nose, and she returned to work a day or two later. But imagine the reactions of coworkers and patients as they saw this new nurse with two huge black eyes and bandages on her face. She wore sunglasses a lot!

Linda can laugh about it now, but she felt mortified at the time. Not exactly the best first impression of one's competence and grace!

I've never had a first-day-on-the-job catastrophe like that one, but I know the perils of a working woman are many! My employment record includes the following:

- Keeping track of the number of jars of kumquat jelly and Poppycock snacks in a department store food shop.

- Keyboarding business documents for executives (whose grammar and spelling aptitudes rated barely above elementary level)—and trying to look indispensable when there wasn't sufficient work to keep even a part-time typist busy.

- Functioning as chief executive officer in charge of domestic tranquillity.

- Searching out, extracting, and implementing monetary-savings vouchers from local and national media sources (clipping coupons).

- Planning and preparing nutrition-rich dietary intake modules and effecting their consumption (making meals and enticing my family to eat them).

- Relentlessly pursuing domestic germ warfare (cleaning the same stuff over and over and over).
- Imparting conflict-resolution skills to younger members of the familial team (keeping my kids from killing each other).
- Direct-sales and tutoring in skills ranging from the delicate art of stained glass to the knotty subject of macramé.
- Creating and fine-tuning (writing and editing) literature for public consumption.
- Making melodic overtures (singing) and addressing public gatherings (speaking and teaching).
- Performing staff-related duties in producing two magazines.

Work is an honorable thing. It keeps us out of mischief, at least most of the time. But no matter what kind of job situation we find ourselves in—whether we work inside the home or out—work often equals stress.

A Working Woman's Stress-a-Day World

Our youngest offspring, who's on her way to a career in restaurant management, always comes home exhausted. "We got slammed tonight," she frequently wails. Though our son is the sports broadcaster, our youngest does a play-by-play of the customers she's had to deal with on her shift. (We've enjoyed these recaps ever since her drive-through-window days at McDonald's when she was fifteen.) The undertippers. The overcranky. The freeloaders who habitually complain about their food until management offers to "comp" a dessert or take

money off their bill. The buxom threesome who keep reposi-
tioning the table so they can all fit into a booth.

On a sadder note, our other daughter remembers the heart-
breaking day she, as a student teacher, had to report a case of
suspected child abuse. Fear for the child's well-being after her
report, fear of reprisals, and fear of having to appear in court—
all brought a great deal of stress.

During my work for the department store food shop, I
myself had many run-ins with a nearing-retirement coworker.
Lizzy had been in her position for two billion years, I think,
and she seemed to think she owned the place.

Because I took the bus to work and Minnesota winters can
wreak havoc on a transit schedule, I would sometimes arrive at
work five or ten minutes late. Having conscientiousness ham-
mered into my head from childhood, I would try to stay five or
ten minutes after 5:00 to make up for my delay. Though she
had no authority to do so, she insisted I clock out at five and be
docked for the time I was late.

There was no pleasing Lizzy. The Monday I faithfully showed
up at work on crutches because I had broken my ankle in a
weekend skiing accident, she ranted about how irresponsible I
was, coming to work like that. By 10:00 I felt like a dishrag and
had to go home. But she acted as though I had broken my
ankle on purpose to somehow increase her workload.

Of course, the day the department head asked me to take
over some of his vacationing secretary's duties, Lizzy erupted in
jealousy because she had more seniority and should have been
asked first. (Never mind that doing two people's work would
have increased her workload.) It took a lot of prayer to get
through my days with Lizzy. But, of course, our family is not
alone in its workplace struggles.

Handling the Stresses

Jeannie, a young seminarian's wife, found that the faster and more efficiently she did her job, the more work her coworkers piled upon her while they dillydallied and shirked their responsibilities. Becoming the butt of her coworkers' jokes, she had to slow down to avoid overwork while they took advantage of her.

Heidi, an experienced teacher, struggled with a new, incompetent principal. "That woman had no idea how to run a school," Heidi says. "I would try to listen to what she said, but I usually wound up doing things my way. God gave me patience (most of the time), but I wish I would have prayed much more for her."

Two women mentioned an even more serious problem. At the age of twenty-two, in her first job, Darla was sexually harassed by her boss several times. Though very scared, she tried to joke her way out of it. "I wish I had been stronger, showed him my anger, and quit," she says.

Julia did find the courage to quit. In her case, managers even witnessed the blatant harassment and simply laughed. Julia then reported the abuse to a female manager. This manager, who had also been sexually harassed there, realized she wasn't the only one, and both she and Julia quit.

A situation like this does call for drastic action. The Bible provides a great example of a person caught in a compromising situation. Joseph—who later became second in power only to the Pharaoh in ancient Egypt—was seduced by Potiphar's wife. Joseph's response? He got out of there. No one has to put up with such reprehensible behavior.

Bringing Integrity to Work

"Integrity," the old saying goes, "is who you are when no one is looking." And the biblical instruction to first-century slaves governs today's workplace as well. A modern paraphrase might read like this: "Employees, sincerely show your employers respect, and honor their authority.... Don't do what's right only when they're watching or only to get a promotion, but work wholeheartedly all the time as though you were serving God Himself in your tasks. You know, the Lord rewards individuals for all the good work they do, whether others notice it or not" (Author's paraphrase of Ephesians 6:5-8).

One woman *lost* a job for standing up for a coworker, but she felt it was the right thing to do. "The employees told me later that the situation improved because of what I did," she says, "and they were grateful I had stepped in for them. I felt vindicated."

Integrity spawns a conscientious work ethic and the determination to do what is right, regardless of the consequences.

Wanda worked for a family-owned business with a perpetually tight cash flow. Her employer asked her to lie about when payments would be mailed. "I went along with it for a while," she admits. But her conscience bothered her. At first she created ways to get around the issue, then simply refused to lie for them. Realizing that the ongoing tension was benefiting neither her nor her employer, she quit her job and moved on.

Bringing Your Faith to Work

"A person in my office is jealous of my knowledge and the advancement I've made on the job," says Terry, an Iowa woman. "She is constantly trying to trip me up or insult me."

Interpersonal problems are always tough to handle. Even the wisest human resources people often can't make much headway in mediating coworker conflicts. And when it's a matter of male-female clashes, employers are only beginning to realize the gender differences in problem solving and communication. "There are definitely differences," says Carol, a staff member at a growing church. "I wish more gender sensitivity training were available and valued."

Both of these women rely on their faith in God, however, to handle office tensions. Carol says, "I have learned to pray, trust God, and not doubt my worth." And when Terry's jealous coworker spouts off, she lets the woman speak, then tries to calmly present her own view, "relying on the Lord for strength," she says. "There's always more you wish you would have said, but there's always next time."

Some women mentioned the reality check of returning to the work force after being home with their young children for several years. "I was shocked at my naiveté," says Jeri, a Missouri mom. "I was unprepared for the terrible language and overall I-don't-care-about-anything attitude. As a secure adult it was hard enough not to get sucked in. I have a new appreciation for how hard it is for our kids to stand up for their beliefs."

Vel, who works with her husband in the real estate business, says her manager felt intimidated by them because he had half their experience. But the manager's mother was a strong Christian, and before she died she told her son, "God put Vel in your office for me." The manager now calls Vel Mom and asks her questions about spiritual things, so Vel is grateful for the position God has given her.

A school food service worker says she wasn't prepared for all the negativism, criticism, and backbiting in the workplace. "I try not to be sucked into all that, but it happens," she says. To combat the problem she tries to practice this scriptural principle: "Whatever is true, whatever is noble, whatever is right, whatever is pure, whatever is lovely, whatever is admirable—if anything is excellent or praiseworthy—think about such things" (Philippians 4:8).

I like the next verse, too. It reinforces the importance of bringing our faith to work. "Whatever you have learned or received or heard from me, or seen in me—put it into practice. And the God of peace will be with you" (v. 9).

Bringing Fun to Work

The most fun I ever had as an employee was in an office in which employees were encouraged to have a good time in their work. Practical jokes abounded—from the disappearing/reappearing plastic lobster (who knows why?) to the office sealed off with yellow "Police Line—Do Not Cross" tape for one woman's thirtieth birthday.

But my favorite time of year was spring break week—complete with a costuming challenge. For one year's contest we were assigned a different season of sports each day, Monday through Thursday, culminating with a Friday noon beach party-picnic, sitting on beach towels on the lunchroom floor.

My competitive, overachiever nature sparked my creativity. I approached Monday's summer theme conservatively. I simply strung two badminton rackets on a silver-tone chain around my neck—one racket hanging down in front, the other in back. Then I wove my silver hoop earrings through a pair of shuttlecocks, which then dangled from each ear.

Spurred on by my coworkers' appreciation of my efforts, Tuesday's fall theme begged for a football get-up. I hauled out my turquoise college alma mater shirt and taped the number fifty on front and back. (The number decorations left over from my husband's fiftieth birthday party. See, Honey? I did use them again someday.) Then I scrounged through the garage to find the rectangular Styrofoam packing pieces that came with my computer and carefully placed them inside my shirt to resemble shoulder pads. For the crowning touch, two pieces of black paper attached with sticky-back tape under my eyes looked just like the gunk the pros use. I had definitely outdone myself!

My coworkers' expectations ran high by Wednesday—the winter theme. I was stymied at first. I don't enjoy winter sports of any kind. They require actually going out into these cold Minnesota winters. I'd rather read a book or watch a movie while snuggled up in front of a cozy fireplace.

But I finally remembered the beautiful pair of white ice skates I had bought when our children were little and I was trying valiantly to avoid passing my "winter dread" on to them. (I wonder why the skates still looked brand new?) Anyway, wearing a slightly-shorter-than-I-usually-wear navy flared skirt with a lace-trimmed cotton pink shell, I used eyebrow pencil to draw lines on my skin to delineate my imaginary flesh-colored body suit. A round neckline and pointed sleeves at the wrists completed the illusion. With a rhinestone tiara atop my head and my skate laces tied together and slung over my shoulders, I dazzled my coworkers with my ice-skating queen masquerade.

By Thursday's spring theme, my resources had run low, but I folded our volleyball net in half several times and wore it around my shoulders as a shawl. With an old, deflated volleyball fitted snugly to my head like a skull cap, my week's worth of costumes garnered a tie for first-place costume honors. You should have seen the other folks' outfits!

You might want to see if you can institute some fun activities at your workplace. But get others to help you organize so you don't have to do everything. My all-time favorite was the indoor miniature golf tournament at the office after work one day. Some of the "holes" required in-and-out-the-elevator putts, moving from floor to floor. Others called for down-the-stairwell shots. Playing in foursomes helped us get to know our coworkers in a relaxed setting, and we laughed a lot!

"A cheerful heart is good medicine," says Proverbs 17:22. When workaday stresses get us down, a little levity—even a little joking around with our fellow employees—can jump-start our tired brains and actually increase our productivity.

But there's more to life than productivity.

Scheduling "Time Out"

A single woman I know quit her job as a college instructor to go into business for herself. After years of classwork and homework to get her bachelor's, master's, and doctoral degrees, then more years of class prep and *grading* homework, she was tired of working so many hours in a day! She had little time to do anything *but* work. No time for friendships. No time for her parents and siblings. No time for renewal. She felt unbalanced. So she began her own business in which she could choose when and how much she would work.

We may not all want to go into business for ourselves. We may need more structure and stability. But we *do* need to make sure we're getting enough time to rest, relax, and refresh.

As an *overachiever* who tends to *overschedule* herself, I've spent a lot of years "flaming the taper at both extremities." I still *overestimate* how much I can do and *underestimate* how long it will take me. But I'm making some progress on pacing myself and taking time to rejuvenate—without feeling guilty! I'm learning that if I don't get tough with myself and get the rest, the days off, and the vacations I need, I'll end up paying later. Payment comes in the form of time lost sick in bed or in the hospital, time lost because I'm too stressed out to think clearly, or time lost because my emotions are in upheaval. It's not worth it.

I guess we need to make sure a Panama hat—a hat of relaxation—graces our millinery wardrobe. We may not be able to take expensive excursions to exotic places, but we do need vacations—real vacations without responsibilities.

We need at least one day of rest each week. Remember, that was one of the original Ten Commandments God gave Moses to help people make sense out of life and to enjoy a good relationship with Him. "You have six days to do all your work, but use the seventh as a day of rest and renewal and devotion to the Lord, your God," He says (Exodus 20:9-10, author's paraphrase).

A ten-minute power nap, a fifteen-minute walk in the fresh air, or a leisurely soak in the tub can ignite enthusiasm for our many tiring tasks. If you have small children, perhaps Dad or a friend could watch them for a few minutes to allow you some restorative personal time.

A Missouri woman who worked outside the home says that she and her husband—who was gone from home a great deal—decided she would have every other Thursday night off. She made dinner for her husband and three children, then left to go out alone for the rest of the evening. "I was free to eat where I wanted to, shop where I wanted to, do what I wanted to—uninterrupted," she says. Time to herself was precious, and looking forward to these outings kept her going on the toughest days.

Yes, we may need to push ourselves for short spurts to accomplish a particular goal or meet a short deadline, but if we continually stretch ourselves too far, we're likely to snap—one way or another.

One woman, who worked evenings and weekends for more than a dozen years to put her husband through school, says there was one time (only one?) when she wanted to "use the rolling pin for something other than what it was intended for." Her husband had said to her, "The reason you don't get things done is that you don't schedule your time properly."

"Can anyone tell me," she asks, "how to schedule incoming phone calls, door-to-door salesmen, unexpected visitors, not to mention sick kids, messy diapers, and car problems? You're ready to leave the house. You've got the diaper bag packed, jackets on the kids, your shopping list in hand, and then you get a whiff of that all-too-familiar smell. It's not just a dirty diaper; it's leaving a trail down the leg into the sock. I don't know about anyone else's babies, but none of mine had bowels that were on any type of set schedule."

Whatever our individual stresses—from impossible bosses to

marathon schedules to feeling like we're being drawn and quartered by our family's demands—we need to find ways to get our necessary rest. A friend reminds me, "God rested on the seventh day of creation and Jesus took time out to rest—even sending people away at times. Why can't we do the same?"

Dilemma: Outside Employment and Motherhood

According to a *Ladies' Home Journal* survey published in the October 1997 issue, the majority of working women said that they're "happy with their dual roles." "And despite the additional responsibilities and challenges they face daily," the article continues, "most wouldn't have it any other way. Sixty-three percent of working women say they would not trade their lifestyle to become stay-at-home moms."[1]

First, I must admit a bias against the term *working women* as opposed to those with outside employment. I once saw a bumper sticker that said, "Mothers *are* working women." I love it! Stay-at-home moms are not *not* working—and most don't bake cookies all day!

Second, even if those statistics are accurate, what about the other 37 percent? That's a big minority.

Third, shortly after I read this article, I mentioned the findings to a group of women at a conference I attended. Sharon, a colleague who teaches high school, edits two magazines, and serves as household strategist (with a husband, two sons, and assorted church responsibilities), responded, "Where do they find these people? I don't know *anybody* who's handling it all well."

Day-care decisions probably cause the greatest dilemma.

Some years ago, a woman with whom my husband worked announced to her fellow employees that she was pregnant with her fourth child in as many years. "Does this mean you'll be quitting your job and staying home with your kids?" a co-worker asked. "Heavens, no [or some more earthy equivalent]," she said. "I couldn't stand being home with my kids all day." One might wonder why she's having all these children in the first place. But surely that mother is in the minority. Most women want what is best for their children and want to be with them as much as possible.

As my cousin Brenda says, "We didn't have these children so somebody else could raise them."

But sometimes extenuating circumstances prevail. Felicia taught in a day-care center and nursery school over a period of twelve years before she and her husband began their family. When their son came along, Felicia desperately wanted to stay home and care for her baby, but financial needs prevented it. Felicia's mom cared for the new baby the first few months, but they needed to make other arrangements. Quality infant care was difficult to find. They felt squeezed between two disappointing alternatives.

Two-parent families often find two incomes the only answer to the realities of today's economy. Many single moms have no choice. And though many working mothers say they would stay home with their children if they could afford to, some feel such satisfaction in their employment that they don't want to put their careers on hold.

At the other end of the spectrum, many working moms today are leaving the work force. From waitresses to TV anchors, women are "taking second looks at hectic lives and making tough decisions about the way they spend their days," write Karen Scalf Linamen and Linda Holland in their book *Working Women, Workable Lives*. "Many are quitting work altogether. Others are dropping to half time or a day or two each week."[2]

So how do you decide what's best for your family?

Weighing All the Factors

A two-paycheck family may tremble at the thought of cutting its income by half. What will they have to give up? Will they be able to keep food on the table? How will they survive?

Financial considerations also dominate *expectant* parents' thoughts. They start pricing coveralls and cradles, swing sets and strollers, Pampers and Pooh bears. Then one glance at their bank balance sends them scrambling for the employment ads.

But for a decision this important, conscientious parents will *together* pray, think through all the options, and ask some tough questions:

1. *Are two jobs better than one?* This may seem like a silly question, but some couples have found that the rising costs of quality child care, coupled with extra expenses incurred when both parents work outside the home, lead to an even bleaker bottom line than when one stayed home.

Elizabeth Johnson discovered this after more than ten years in the workplace. According to her April 1991 *Redbook* article, she thought her love of her job, happy one-year-old baby, and supportive husband spelled success. But a visit to their accountant brought bad news.

"We were losing money, even though we were both working

full-time," she writes. "After that meeting it became extremely difficult for me to justify my job, no matter how gratifying I found it, when it took me away from my daughter fifty hours a week *and made no improvement in our financial situation.*"[3]

You might want to make a list of the financial gains and losses involved if you both work outside the home. Be honest, and figure expenses on the high side. Expenses often exceed projections.

2. *Does Mom really* **need** *to work outside the home?* Deborah Fallows, former assistant dean at Georgetown University and now full-time mom, says, "The 'need' to work varies enormously from person to person and often depends less on straightforward economic pressure than on material desires and individual definitions of success."[4]

Mom's *working outside the home* often demands sacrifices from every member of the family—perhaps parents missing a special preschool celebration, fewer or shorter times for cuddling before bedtime, shorter hours for sleep, or giving up leisure time to help with household chores.

Mom's *staying home to raise the children* may also demand sacrifices—perhaps a smaller home, moving to a neighborhood or region of the country with a lower cost of living, taking less-expensive vacations, cooking from scratch, sewing some of your family's clothes, or shopping at garage sales more than department stores.

Yet sacrifice is a stranger to most moms and dads today. We've been told we can have it all. And some believe it!

In his book *Women Leaving the Workplace*, Larry Burkett relates the story of Barbara, a woman who couldn't stand the sacrifices needed to reenter the work force. She said, "I found myself crying each morning on my way to work as I left my sleeping babies, knowing that I wouldn't even touch them ... until 6:00 P.M. (or later), dragging my tired self in from a very busy workday at the office which had been inevitably followed by a hectic drive across town in late afternoon traffic."

After much soul searching, Barbara gave up her $30,000-a-year salary with fear and trembling to stay home with her children. "However, when we truly needed something, I prayed, and the Lord always answered," she says. "On one occasion when I had been praying for children's clothing, I received so much [from friends cleaning out closets or noticing the right sizes at garage sales] that on one night when my husband arrived home from work, he literally could not walk through the living room for all the stacks and boxes of clothes. He looked at me and calmly asked, 'You've been praying again, haven't you?'"[5]

We don't hear many stories of God's provision anymore. Are we depriving our children of faith-building lessons in God's faithfulness?

3. *Does Mom really **want** to work outside the home?* Some women, especially those with well-established careers, want to work after they've had a baby. They have spent four or more years in college, perhaps, preparing for a vocation, and they enjoy their work. In our society, work often defines who we are.

But a mother who doesn't *want* to work outside the home, and does it, often projects her misgivings onto her children, who in turn have more difficulty adjusting to day-care situations. Likewise, a mother who feels trapped at home may also project those feelings onto her husband or children. A mom who wants to stay home with her children should not feel second-class or undervalued. Parenting requires wisdom, patience, and a variety of skills. So we need to be honest with our feelings and work through them with a lot of prayer.

Listen to your heart in these matters. "Delight yourself in the Lord and he will give you the desires of your heart" (Psalm 37:4). Not only will He give us the desires *of* our heart but also *for* our heart. But first, we need to delight ourselves in Him. If we're spending time with God, listening to Him, discussing our desires and needs—personal and financial—He has promised to lead us.

If our desire to continue our career is from the Lord, He will help us discover creative ways to maximize the time with our children. Job sharing, flexible time schedules, and telecommuting are becoming more common as women explore the possibilities.

If our desire to stay home is from Him, God will help us find ways to make ends meet and to feel fulfilled in that choice.

4. *Will there be enough time and energy left for involvement in church and community activities that are important to us?* List your priorities and values. Prayerfully consider where working outside the home fits in the big picture. Both working in a secular environment and socializing with other mothers in our neighborhoods can create opportunities to tell others about our faith in Christ. But we need to be careful not to exceed our energy limit.

5. *How will we instill and nurture Christian values in our children?* Make sure your care provider shares your values and beliefs or at least is not antagonistic to them. Then live in

Deuteronomy 6:6–7: "These commandments that I give you today are to be upon your hearts. Impress them on your children. Talk about them when you sit at home and when you walk along the road, when you lie down and when you get up."

During precious moments with your children talk about the God who created the butterfly you see on your walk or emphasize the two-sided coin of love that disciplines. Bedtimes are especially tender times to turn conversation to spiritual insights.

6. *Are there other options?*

a. Consider downsizing—moving to a smaller house, selling nonessentials such as a boat, second car, or electronic equipment. Create a leaner budget and stick to it. When finances get tight at our house, my husband and I adopt what we call our "Austerity Budget." It's tough to stick to sometimes. But, as one woman said, "With each potential purchase we have to ask ourselves, 'Is this really a *necessity?*'"

b. Consider working at home. No one said it was easy, but cottage industries—everything from crafts to word processing to light assembly work—are experiencing a remarkable comeback.

The mom who balances employment with caring for her kids inside the home enjoys a more flexible schedule, relaxed dress code, and the ability to choose her workload. But often she also struggles with discipline, distractions, and diminished or irregular paychecks.

My sister Jan, who runs her own sewing business, admits, "It's easy to procrastinate, friends and family may not take your work time seriously, and you can never lock your business door and go home."

Pam Chambers can relate. She was delighted when she could opt for "telecommuting," the opportunity to work out of her home. "Much of my time is spent on the phone and doing paperwork," she says. But the balancing act proved more difficult than expected. "Baby needs a dirty diaper changed. I begin changing the baby on the floor. Older child falls. I dash for ice and the phone rings. I run to answer. It's an important client. Baby crawls away naked, leaving a trail everywhere."

And then there are the times when you need to concentrate and the kids need you. One of the most discouraging times in my writing came when a dozen rejection slips appeared in my mailbox over a short period of time. A writer friend sent me a card with the drawing of a little girl with big dark eyes, saying, "Now is no time to stop writing." Encouraged by her thoughtfulness, I pinned the card on my bulletin board.

One day, while I thought our kids were playing semipeacefully in the yard, I tried to concentrate on a project. Suddenly my middle child's little voice startled me. "I don't know about that," she said.

"What don't you know about?" I asked, barely looking up from my work.

"That thing says, 'Now is no time to stop writing,'" she said, pointing to the bulletin board. "I don't know about that."

She had my full attention. I knew that she needed a little time with Mom. I was glad I was there. But I also had to make up that time later.

c. Consider being the child-care provider yourself. Other parents, like you, are searching for someone who understands their predicament. What an opportunity for Christian women (and men)! God's love in your life will spill over in the way you love the children, and their parents will notice. Besides, you'll get paid for staying home with your kids!

Everybody Pulling Together

No matter what your family situation, if you don't want your many hats tumbling down around your feet, it's important to find a support team. Here are some ideas for strengthening family cooperation:

- Cultivate relationships with other Christians for emotional support. Everyone needs friends who will listen, encourage, and share experiences.

- If you're married, invest time in building your marriage as well. Keep dating your spouse so you don't become strangers as you each fulfill your many roles.

- Don't "let things slide." Life is too short and children grow too quickly.

- Give the gift of cooperation. Though in general today's men help more at home, women still do the majority of the cooking, cleaning, and child care. If both parents work outside the home, they and the children—as they're able—need to look for ways to help each other keep the home running smoothly.

Above all, we need to avoid judging others for their work and family choices and pray for a discerning heart when sifting through others' advice to us. Jenna said she asked a neighbor woman to watch her children for a few hours one day because Jenna and her husband's work schedules overlapped that day. The neighbor declined, saying she didn't think it was right for a woman to work outside the home, so she didn't think she should baby-sit for a woman who was, Jenna recalls. Although the neighbor changed her mind and apologized a few years later, she had demoralized Jenna and left her stranded.

"And over all [the] virtues put on love, which binds them all together in perfect unity" (Colossians 3:14).

Wearing the Working Woman's Hat—With Style

"I love being able to let God create in me 'His woman,'" says Pam from Iowa. "Sometimes it's a mama full of kisses and hugs. Sometimes it's a teacher caring for thirty at once. Sometimes it's a wife giving my whole being to my husband. Sometimes it's an individual—exercising, reading, pampering myself. My job is to let God be the Creator of my life—rather than trying to create myself."

Our joys of being a woman (and, perhaps, a mother) and our joys in our work—whether at home or "abroad" (outside the home)—may conflict often. But if we prayerfully think through the trade-offs, keep family needs foremost, and ask God to help us manage our many hats of work, He promises to be with us in every detail.

The wise and noble working woman "is clothed with strength and dignity; she can laugh at the days to come," says the proverb writer. "A woman who fears the Lord is to be praised. Give her the reward she has earned, and let her works bring her praise" (Proverbs 31:25, 30-31). Remember, it was more than her work that won her praise. Above all it was her fear of the Lord!

Still, it's through our relationships that we can find the help we need from time to time....

Study Questions

1. Most of us work—whether at home or outside the home (abroad). Work is an honorable thing, not a curse, but it usually requires us to deal with other human beings, which often brings conflict. How do 1 Corinthians 4:12-14 and Colossians 3:14 help us deal with these realities?

2. Read Ephesians 6:5-8. Since the slave-master relationship mentioned here could apply to the employee-employer relationship of today, write out a paraphrase of these verses for today's workplace. Whether or not you work outside the home, how might you paraphrase this verse to find a proper mindset in the work you do for your family?

3. Read Philippians 4:7-9. How might this "mind discipline" help in our work? How can you put this idea into practice this week? What benefit does God promise with this discipline?

4. Read Proverbs 17:22. How do you think this bit of wisdom can help us maintain a good mindset in the workplace or as we work at home?

5. Read Proverbs 31:13-27. This virtuous woman (and Scripture says a woman like this is hard to find) seems to be able to juggle both home and business with amazing efficiency and love. But as she takes care of all her career responsibilities, how do we know she maintains a healthy commitment to her family's needs? Now read verse 30. Above all, for what does she deserve praise? How do you suppose she finds the strength to do all she does?

6. Read Exodus 20:8-10. This commandment is repeated often in both the Old Testament and the New Testament. What are some possible ways this commandment could be seen as God's demonstrating His love for us? What are some ways you can make one day a week—probably Sunday (the Lord's Day)—more special and restful?

For overachievers or those needing extra encouragement, look up these verses: 1 Chronicles 28:20; 2 Chronicles 15:7; Proverbs 14:23 and 18:9; 1 Corinthians 15:58; 2 Corinthians 9:8 and Colossians 3:23. What stands out most to you personally as an encouragement or a little "nudge" regarding your work?

FIVE

Caroline Ingalls, Will You Tie My Sunbonnet?

~

My Role as a Daughter (and Daughter-in-Law)

My relationship with my parents is growing from tension to bonding with love.

—Janet Hawkinson
Her hats include those of school
food service worker, wife of a computer
drafting technician, mother of
two married daughters.

Joking about her mom's sometimes incomprehensible behavior, my niece will say with a twinkle in her eye, "Mom, when the little men in white coats show up—just go."

Don't you sometimes wish for the *Little House on the Prairie* warmth—the parent-child closeness and mutual understanding that oozed from that idyllic TV show?

Several years ago, during summer vacation, Meagan tried to organize a family game of softball. No one wanted to play. They grumbled and stalled and made up excuses. Frustrated, Meagan struck a hands-on-hips position. "Wouldn't it be nice to play a game together like they do on *The Cosby Show?*" she pleaded.

"*The Cosby Show* isn't real life," her son piped up. "Real life is

Christmas with Nana Elsie." Meagan wasn't sure how her son's logic jumped from softball to the most cantankerous member of the family, but he did put TV fantasies into perspective.

As an adult woman, relationships with parents (our kids' sweet, adored grandparents) can be some of the most difficult. I believe that trying to understand our parents may rival trying to understand men!

Some parents' depression-era mentality compels them to hoard every plastic food container, rubber band, twist-tie, and fast-food salt packet that ever sneaked into their house. Such delightful treasures might be needed someday.

Some parents can't stand the thought of change: "If it was good enough for us when we were raising our kids, it's good enough for the next generation."

Some parents, discontented with the way their own lives turned out, inflict pain by trying to spare their children pain.

Snipping the apron ties—as if anyone wears aprons anymore—has always required the delicate skill of a surgeon.

Typically in adolescence we try everything from hunger strikes to disappearing acts in protest of our parents' because-I-said-so rules and "otherplanetary" expectations. (Then we watch with awe as a younger sibling twists those rules and our once-rigid parents into pinky-wrapping pretzels.)

After we declare our own private Independence Day, we may nod occasionally in our parents' direction, but we're "establishing ourselves" and, perhaps, establishing families of our own. Often that's when we begin to suspect that our parents had human blood flowing through their veins after all. We may actually impose some of the same rules on our children, perhaps trying to serve up more palatable reasons than "Because I said so."

But we also discover that the flip side of "Once a parent, always a parent," is "Once a child, always a child"—at least in our parents' eyes.

Still Their Little Girl

A single woman told me that driving her elderly parents to family functions makes her feel totally inept. "I don't like being told how to drive and where to turn," she says. "They are the ones who taught me. It feels like a challenge, that I can't do it, and that to them I'm still a child."

A college professor named Kathy describes the most difficult time in her relationship with her parents. When she was a young wife and teacher expecting her first child, she and her husband moved to her hometown after several years away. They had bought a house, and Kathy planned to stay home to care for their new little one. But financial complications and legal battles on the seller's end left the young couple with no place to live. Kathy's parents invited their daughter and son-in-law to stay with them until the matter was settled. It seemed a good arrangement.

Then Kathy lost the baby.

Because she had no job, Kathy grieved at home alone all day while her husband and parents worked. Her dad kept giving her "pointers" on how to find employment (as though she had never gone through the procedure before). Her mom left to-do lists of chores to accomplish while everyone else was gone. They thought they were helping. (Parents long to fix things for their kids, don't they?) But Kathy felt smothered and used. Her grieving process only deepened.

No baby. No house. No life of her own.

In her parents' eyes, she was still their little girl. Mom and Dad slipped into the familiar roles they had enjoyed before she was married.

Her grief brought her to a crisis point in her faith, she says. "It came down to the bottom line: Do I believe there is a God or don't I? Do I believe He loves me or don't I?" Though she had begun a personal relationship with Jesus Christ years earlier, this was its first major test. Without her faith in God, Kathy says, she's not sure how she could have endured the stress. In retrospect, she believes that she and her husband and parents could have avoided some of their difficulties by sitting down together to talk through each other's expectations, feelings, and needs.

Most women I've talked to who have tried to live with their parents or in-laws after marriage agree that two women under one roof spells trouble. I think that's why God, in His great wisdom, says that a married person is to leave parents to unite with the new spouse (see Genesis 2:24). Each family needs autonomy yet lovingly maintained ties to the rest of the extended family.

Whether we live near or far from our parents, a spouse (or even a close friend) can often help us maintain perspective on that constantly changing relationship with parents. Even thousands of miles away, we can feel captive to their expectations.

Choice Words—and Actions

A father's perfectionism and a mother's apparent ease at juggling many responsibilities—when the daughter can't measure up on either score—could paralyze her. Offhanded comments about mildew behind the shower curtain or even a disapproving look regarding the daughter's choice of disciplinary measures can make her feel like never inviting her parents to visit again.

A woman might blame her personality or current problems on parental abuse or manipulation, on being underloved or overindulged. A young woman once told me she couldn't change a certain behavior. "That's just the way I am," she said. But I believe God holds each of us accountable for what we allow to control our lives. We can choose to be victims or choose to trust God to help us make needed changes.

None of us had perfect parents. Some parents have made mistakes that changed the course of our lives. Some have committed hideous sins against us. Some showed us little affection, perhaps because no one modeled it for them. These may be *reasons* for some of our personal problems, but they're not *excuses* for refusing to make necessary changes.

Every day we make a choice. We can let bitter resentment gnaw at our hearts and snatch away our joy, or we can choose to forgive as Jesus Christ has forgiven our sins against Him. "Be kind and compassionate to one another," the Bible says—and that includes parents—"forgiving each other, just as in Christ God forgave you" (Ephesians 4:32).

My mother-in-law illustrated this for me in a beautiful way. Marianne's relationship with her parents had been strained since her teens. She ran away from home, got married, and didn't see her parents for years. My husband and his siblings never even met their maternal grandparents until their school years, when their grandmother was hospitalized with a broken hip.

In the interim, Marianne and her husband, Harold, had

learned of Jesus Christ's love for them and began following Him. Though her parents'—especially her father's—offenses and hurts had burrowed deep, Marianne and Harold learned how to forgive.

By the time I met them, Marianne's mother, Mattie—nearly ninety years old—lived in a nursing home on the edge of town. Every day Marianne went out to fix her mother's hair, feed her, and help with other care needs.

Knowing their history, I was impressed with Marianne's tender care. But her faithfulness grew even more remarkable. Due to Alzheimer's or dementia, Mattie began accusing her daughter of treating her badly and stealing personal items. Mattie often lashed out in rage and threatened to call the sheriff.

Marianne would come home in tears. But the next day she would return to the nursing home to help her mother. Marianne's faith in Christ, forgiving spirit, love, and sense of responsibility brought her back day after day, regardless of how her mother responded. What a beautiful example!

Love, Honor, and Obey

Although the words *love, honor,* and *obey* appear in some traditional wedding ceremonies, I believe they encapsulate the Bible's instructions for our relationship with our parents. As previously mentioned, "Love one another" includes that couple that brought us into the world. And they need to hear us express our love in both actions and words.

One mom complained that her young adult son never said he loved her or his dad. She would end phone conversations with "I love you," but the son would reply, "OK, bye," or some other noncommittal parting. Her husband also had difficulty verbally expressing his love to their kids and his parents, and she encouraged him to speak those three important words.

Then one day, as she ended a phone conversation with her own parents, she realized that she hadn't made a habit of expressing her love to them, either. For some reason it was easier to tell her husband and children she loved them than to tell her parents. So she began making a conscious effort to remind them of her love.

But what about *honoring* and *obeying*? As we mature, our responsibility to obey our parents' edicts grows into one of respecting their lives and their wishes. It's not always easy. But I believe the old Golden Rule shines brightest here: "So in everything, do to others what you would have them do to you" (Matthew 7:12).

I once heard author Tony Campolo speak about taking his children to see their elderly grandparents regularly—to visit and do things for them. Why? "Because I want them to know how I want to be treated when I get old," he said.

My own childhood memories include periodic Sunday afternoon trips to a nursing home to see my great-grandmother. Diabetes ravaged her body, requiring the amputation of both legs. But I'll never forget her smile whenever we came.

A few years later, when my grandfather died, my parents bought a different house to give Grandma her own apartment yet make her a part of our lives. Those early impressions molded within me a deep respect, concern, and care for family—especially the elderly.

We may not always agree with our parents' wishes, and we may not always follow their advice, but honor and respect minimize the static in communication lines. A good relationship with parents can also help us work together in handling our many hats of responsibility.

Clearing the Air

Some families struggle more than others. And the barbs of parent-child relationships are often pointed on both ends. In the awkward process of becoming independent, we may have wounded our parents more than we know.

Several years into my marriage, I realized that I, like many young people, hadn't handled the independence transition very well. In high school I announced to my parents where I wanted to go to college and what I wanted to do with my life. They weren't bad choices. But typically self-absorbed, I didn't seek my parents' counsel or give them a chance to express an opinion.

After I was married, I began feeling I had dishonored them. They never said anything, but I wanted to eliminate any possible barriers between us. My mother was in the hospital with a heart ailment at the time, and I didn't know how much longer we would have her with us. Summoning all my courage (and with the support of my husband), I went to my mom's hospital room. I asked forgiveness from both of my parents for not being more sensitive to their guidance while I was still at home.

With forgiveness given and received, I sensed we moved to another level in our relationship that night.

As it turned out, my mother is still with us. I didn't get to college until age thirty-nine, after I had raised three children to relative maturity. And I didn't follow the career path I thought I would. But that wasn't the point. The relationship was more important than the outcome.

Now as my own children have reached adulthood, they have taught me a great deal about maturing. Adolescents often think they prove their maturity by asserting their independence—making decisions completely on their own. But we knew our kids were becoming mature when they progressed from acting independently to seeking our counsel. We, as parents, then could transition from *rulemakers* to *peers* whose opinions they respected—at least most of the time.

Time—and Time Again

When asked what they do to maintain a good relationship with their parents, a few of my survey respondents said, "Learned to hold my tongue." I love it! I don't think that's necessarily suppressing anger. I think it can be a healthy exercise of self-control, one of the characteristics of a person who is letting God's Holy Spirit control her life (see Galatians 5:22-23). Holding a tongue is turning the situation over to God and letting Him handle it, rather than churning inside or exploding.

Others offered more active means of maintaining the relationship: making phone calls, sending letters (as well as cards, e-mail, photos, and videos), working on projects together, vacationing together, inviting them to their grandchildren's big moments (sports, drama, music), listening, thanking them, and appreciating them. But the key words were *spending time*.

One woman said, "I try to carve out time to make trips home." It takes major surgery on our schedules sometimes to find that time, doesn't it? But there's nothing like having children of our own to remind us how much our parents invested in us.

When our daughter was pregnant, her dad and I accompanied her to one of her prenatal classes. The first order of business that evening was a reality check of how much time it takes to care for a newborn. If you count feeding, bathing, diapering, comforting the baby when it cries, playing, and all the other little ways a parent interacts with the child, the estimated grand total comes to about twelve to fifteen hours a day. That's a big time investment, and that's just the first few months!

Worth the Sacrifice

They may not say it in the sweetest way sometimes, but our parents simply don't want to be forgotten. Would we? One of the best ways we can honor their sacrifices for us is **to re**pay dividends—of time—on their investment. Yes, we're busy. They know that. And that's what makes the moments we can spend with them even more precious.

For many years my husband and I lived within a mile of my parents' house, and we would often pass nearby while running errands or coming home from other outings. "Let's stop by Grandma and Grandpa's just to say 'Hi,'" we would suggest to our kids. It became a family joke, however, because "just saying 'Hi'" almost always took several hours—with our kids falling asleep on the sofa or floor.

Sometimes elderly parents can't take a large dose of family—especially if the kids are a little too active for them. One woman said she and her husband now get a motel room when they go back home to visit parents so they can catch up on each other's lives in shorter, less stressful snatches.

Another woman found the motel routine necessary earlier in her family's life because the in-laws, on their own turf, became harshly controlling with the grandchildren.

One time-management expert recommends scheduling time with parents—and children and husband—just as you would a doctor or dental appointment. Some of us function more spontaneously, but whatever our approach, we need to *make* the time. We never know how long we will have our parents with us.

When my mom had a stroke more than twenty years ago, she was paralyzed on one side for several weeks. Not having realized how difficult it would be to see her like that, I expressed my frustrations to God through a bit of free verse:

A mother is someone strong:
She can tell you how to stretch a pound of hamburger
or a yard of material,
someone who can read a story to your children
or play a game to entertain them.
But what about when the speech is incoherent,
the logic is askew,
and the simplest game rules become complicated?
When I'm impatient, forgive me.
Heal my attitude
while her body recuperates.
And if she is to remain this way,
teach me how to make it easier for her.

No matter how tarnished the relationship has become with our parents up to this point, God created within us a built-in tenderness for them. With a little polish of love, forgiveness, and time, we can cherish the shining beauty of that relationship. And then when our parents are gone, we can smile at their memory.

Remember, one of Jesus' last concerns—as He gave His life for us—was for the care of His mother (see John 19:25-27).

Run-Ins With In-Laws

Are you a victim of pentheraphobia? That's the fear of your mother-in-law.

Despite the fact that many women enjoy good relationships with their in-laws, the jokes have embedded themselves in our culture. And true horror stories abound—stories of controlling in-laws, nit-picky criticism, bitter jealousy when kids spend holidays with "the other parents," demanding in-laws, bad investments with their children's money, and miscommunication. (Lord, keep me from being one of those types!)

Perhaps because opposites attract, marriages often bind together two families who otherwise never would have been friends.

One woman said the best way to handle in-laws is to live two thousand miles away. How sad! To cut ourselves off deprives us of the richness we can draw from the two families. But beginning a new family with its own lifestyle, its own traditions, its own autonomy, while maintaining an honoring, respectful relationship with the parents and in-laws sometimes seems like dreaming the impossible dream.

One woman attended a multiethnic church with her

husband and children, so she struggled with in-laws who, even while around the kids, used pejorative terms for minorities. Another got upset when her father-in-law used profanity in front of her toddler. Another struggled because her in-laws didn't understand the commitment to Jesus Christ she and her husband had made. "They thought their son had been brainwashed," she says.

Learning when to speak and when to hold our tongues sometimes takes extraordinary wisdom. But these women responded in interesting ways.

Though they felt awkward, woman number one and her husband talked with the offending parents and explained their sensitivity to racial remarks. Living in a small town and not well-educated, the parents hardly knew any minorities. They merely echoed the sentiments of others around them. After their little talk the occasional slip usually was followed by an apology.

Mother number two admits she lashed out when her father-in-law swore. Trying to manage a joking tone, she scolded, "If he ever says that word, I'm going to wash *your* mouth out with soap!" Not the most diplomatic approach, but it worked. "After that, [my father-in-law] didn't swear at all around the kids until they were grown," she says.

Woman number three says her relationship with her family has improved but only because others in the family have come to know Jesus Christ. They've seen this isn't brainwashing. It's a totally new life, clean and meaningful because of Christ's love.

Sometimes a memorized verse of Scripture can help us get through the tension spots with in-laws:

- Under criticism, we can repeat over and over, "Great peace have they which love thy law: and nothing shall offend them" (Psalm 119:165, KJV).

- When they think they're always right—and they're not—we can remind ourselves, "Blessed are the peacemakers" (Matthew 5:9).

- Faced with their irritating habits, insensitivity, and intrusiveness, we can work through our own irritability and faults by mulling this over: "The wisdom that comes from heaven is first of all pure; then peace-loving, considerate, submissive, full of mercy and good fruit, impartial and sincere. Peacemakers who sow in peace raise a harvest of righteousness" (James 3:17-18).

Endearing Yourself to Your In-Laws

Whether newly married or deeply entrenched in battles with in-laws, we can all improve or enhance these relationships by remembering a few practical points.

1. Remember: You can catch more flies with honey than with vinegar. Someone has to be the first one to show love. It's your move. It's the feelings-follow-action principle. Love is something you do. Take the initiative in planning family get-togethers (unless that's your mother-in-law's favorite thing to do—then let her do it). Be thoughtful in buying gifts. Find areas in which you can compliment your "second family."

The first idea may be easier for those of us whose husbands treat the family social calendar like an infectious disease, leaving all the planning details to their wives. Thoughtful gift giving may be almost second nature for the born-to-shop woman—if we don't take the attitude, "She's *your* mother. Why should *I* have to buy her gift!" Try to pick up on your in-laws' interests, tastes, and subtle hints they may or may not realize they're dropping.

Giving compliments? That can be tough if the relationship is strained. But Jean Miller, a Texas woman, discovered fringe benefits to sincere compliments. "Instead of tuning her out (instinctive reaction), I decided to placate Mom Miller by acknowledging her authority on one subject—cooking. I ask her for recipes and beg for menu suggestions. This satisfies her need to feel important, and she now intrudes much less on other areas of my life."[1]

Be careful not to go overboard, though. Early in my marriage, trying to win my mother-in-law's favor, I raved about a particular cookie she made. It *was* good, but thereafter, every time we visited her or she sent Christmas packages, she deluged us with tons of those cookies.

2. Remember: Most weaknesses have a flip side of strength. The flip side of stubbornness can be perseverance under impossible situations. The flip side of a controlling nature can be tenacious devotion and loving care. And even if we can't find the positive flip side to what appears a weakness in our in-law's personality, sometimes we can help develop it.

Danielle, a can't-sit-still, high-energy woman, decided to help one of her mother-in-law's weaknesses become a strength. "My husband's mom comes from 'frumpy, outdated, dead, small-town, USA,'" she says. "I never wanted to visit her and sit there and hear all about nothing. For my husband's sake, I forced myself to get interested in her and help make her life more exciting. I started doing 'big-city' stuff for her, buying her new books, redecorating her old apartment, taking her to shows and out to eat. This kept me interested and has totally 'wowed up' her life. She is much more exciting to be with now, and my husband is *very* grateful."

We may not always get such a positive response to our efforts to do an in-law makeover, but a positive attitude and genuine interest in them can often transform their attitude toward us.

3. Remember: Keep your home a safe haven for you and your family. One woman says, "I have been so sensitive about my in-laws' suggestions on child-rearing, marriage relationships, cooking, and everything, that I felt they were critical, and I didn't like being around them. I strongly guard my conversations with them so that everything will appear to be more than perfect."

But our family is to be our haven—a safe place to relax and be ourselves. Allowing our parents or in-laws that much control over us is not healthy. And it can be confusing for our children to observe. One woman put up with criticism and thoughtless "dropping in without notice" for years before she finally had the courage to speak up. Being careful to speak in "I" terms (expressing how these offenses made her feel), rather than "you" terms (blaming), she lovingly confronted her in-laws. In response, they apologized with a "We didn't realize …" then admitted to some hurt feelings of their own, which both couples ironed out together in time.

"It's not just *what* you do in a relationship that matters, it's *who* you are," she writes. "And being yourself, I've learned, means being able to stand up for your wishes and feelings."[2]

It's not a matter here of insisting on our rights. It's a matter of being honest about things that hurt us.

4. Remember: Peacemaking is better than peacekeeping.
Though our natural tendency can be to sweep things under the rug or to complain to other family members about difficulties in our relationships with parents-in-law, it's better to "get rid of the dirt" altogether so you don't keep tripping over that ever-growing carpet lump. Even siblings-in-law can get trapped. Holly, a young Minnesota mom, said older siblings kept trying to get her and her husband to influence the parents, to sway them to their way of thinking. But Holly refuses to become a Ping-Pong ball in the relationship game of life. "They worry too much, and they're too bossy," she says.

It may not be easy, but these are the kinds of things families need to talk out instead of letting them fester.

5. Remember: You can disagree without disrespect. It has been said that if two people agree on absolutely everything, one of them is not necessary. Yet arguing solves little. In fact, it usually makes the situation worse. I like the way my grandfather paraphrased part of an old Samuel Butler poem: "A man convinced against his will is of the same opinion still." If morality is not at issue, compromise may be our best ally. But keeping a healthy respect for in-laws can smooth potential porcupine-quill areas. No matter how ornery in-laws may seem at times, they can't be all bad; after all, they produced the husband we love! And it's especially important not to tarnish their image in the eyes of our children—their grandchildren.

6. Remember: The Golden Rule applies to in-laws, too. If we truly treated our in-laws as we would like to be treated, I believe many of our conflicts would vanish. Love, kindness, thoughtfulness—even communicating our hurts—it all goes both ways. We have the power to set a positive, loving tone in our relationship rather than reacting in hurt or anger to negatives. It's a choice. Jesus said all the commandments and biblical instruction can be summed up in that glistening Golden Rule.

But many times dealing with parents or in-laws is only half the story.

A Pickle Sandwich

I like the term *sandwich generation,* describing the plight of those who feel smooshed between adolescent or young adult children and aging parents. Add a slice of menopause, and you've got a real "hero" sandwich. It might be teens—rebellious, floundering, or overcommitted. It could be adult children—trapped in webs of painful relationships or habits. But that hat of concern constantly weighs on our heads. As our parents' minds or health deteriorate, more heaviness bogs us down.

We, as women, feel it much more keenly than our male counterparts, it seems. Our sensitive, nurturing spirit wants to make everyone happy and comfortable.

A woman named Mary says that when her youngest child was twelve, Mary and her husband took his parents in to live with them. "Both were in very poor health," she says. "We would do it again, but it was a critical age for my preteen, and it put our whole family under stress. My mother-in-law was very difficult and self-centered. We should have found more ways for the twelve-year-old to feel important."

A former coworker of mine says the sandwich generation can also apply to single women squeezed between their careers and their responsibility for their parents. "There's guilt in knowing how much time and energy should be given to their care. Is more expected from me because I don't have responsibilities for adolescents like my sibling does?"

One way she and her sister are trying to work out their dilemma is that her sister provides for the physical needs around the house. My friend helps with the emotional support. But sometimes the emotional is far more difficult to wrestle with than the physical, so my friend is trying to find that fragile balance.

Yet Another Layer?

Perhaps the term *club sandwich* could best describe the woman wedged between husband, career, adult children, and parents.

While I was working on this book, a friend introduced me to Karen—the faculty secretary at a Christian college. My friend told her about the 500 hats theme of my book and specifically the sandwich generation topic. Tears welled in Karen's eyes. "Do you know where I've just been?" she asked. "Putting my parents on a plane to California."

As we talked further, her story tumbled out. Her frail, elderly parents had been visiting for a month. At the same time, one of her daughters was going through a divorce, so the grandchildren spent a lot of time with Grandma and Grandpa.

As understanding as her boss at the college was, Karen simply could not let her responsibilities there slide, either. It was hard to say good-bye to her parents, sending them back to no one but their son with Down Syndrome. The parents' leaving brought both concern and relief.

When asked how she handles it all, Karen said simply, "With a lot of prayer." She talked about the prayers of the single adult group at church that she and her husband lead. She talked about other women at work in similar situations who pray with her and offer emotional support. She talked about the therapeutic value of work, to help her keep life in perspective and her mind off all the sadness.

Another friend offered, "I don't think you handle it as much as get through it."

The Little Men in White Coats?

Sometimes we do feel we're going to become a mental case, dealing with all these heavy concerns at once. Worst-case scenarios hover over our daytime thoughts and haunt our nightmares.

Over the past several years, as my husband and I took each of our kids, in turn, to the college campuses of their choice, a little seed of fear embedded itself in my mind. I worried about the temptations and evil influences all around them. How would they hold up? I wondered. But ultimately I had to entrust them into God's care. I knew I couldn't hold their sweaty little hands and walk them to every class. (Wouldn't they have loved that!)

The day one of our children admitted to a problem I hoped

I would never have to face, I truly understood the meaning of the words *heavy heart.* I felt I had to drag mine around with me everywhere I went. I tried to turn my thoughts into prayers, but sometimes I had to ask the Lord to take over in that department because I didn't even know how to pray for the situation.

I don't think men dwell on the painful things as we tend to do. They seem to be able to compartmentalize their lives more. Our Creator has given women the tender ability to care, and though it seems a curse at times, it's one of my favorite parts of being a woman.

Though seldom easy, nurturing our relationships with our parents and in-laws while dealing with families and careers of our own is actually one way to bring more balance to our leaning tower of many hats. Our parents and in-laws are more than occasional baby-sitting service, and a give-and-take relationship can draw upon their experience and wisdom. We will definitely need it, especially when the roles reverse and we need to parent our parents.

All the while we can draw strength and compassion and love from our God who created us this way. And He put us in families and communities to draw strength and compassion from each other....

Study Questions

1. Read Genesis 2:24. How might the leaving and uniting principles in this verse indicate that our all-knowing, all-wise God cares about human relationships, including family relationships after marriage? How can we guard our individual new family unit yet lovingly maintain ties to the rest of our extended family? What are some ways you, with God's help, have handled the sometimes unrealistic expectations of parents and in-laws?

2. Read Luke 18:20 and Ephesians 6:2-3. What sins does Jesus lump together with not honoring mothers and fathers? What benefit does God promise to those who honor their parents? Obviously, some who have been very good to their parents have not lived to old age, so what do you think this promise means?

3. Read Ephesians 4:31-32. How do you think these verses could apply to our relationships with parents and in-laws?

4. Read Matthew 7:12. As a woman matures and perhaps has children of her own, she may begin to understand her parents better. How do you think this "Golden Rule" of Scripture applies to this phenomenon? How can it guide our responses to difficult parents or in-laws?

5. Read Galatians 5:22-23. What is the all-important source of these good character qualities, essential in good human relationships?

6. Read John 19:25-27. What was one of Jesus' last concerns as He gave His life for us on the cross?

7. Read Psalm 119:165 (in the King James Version if possible), Matthew 5:9, and James 3:17-18. What mind attitudes and outward actions do these verses encourage us to develop? How can they help us enjoy better relationships?

SIX

Is My Halo On Straight?

My Role in God's Family

I appreciate how God has created women ... especially our propensity for putting a high priority on relationships.

—Carol Madison
Her hats include those of director of adult
and children's ministries in her church, member
of servant leadership team for the Celebrate Jesus
2000 movement in Minneapolis/St. Paul,
Minnesota, member of the Midwest
Concerts of Prayer board of directors.

My Aunt Lucy was discussing heaven with her young daughter as they drove along in the car one day. "Heaven is a place where everyone will be happy," Lucy said. "There won't be any spankings or crying there."

"Isn't Daddy going to be there?" her daughter replied.

The ultimate in happiness, from a child's viewpoint, may be the abolishment of spankings—or those responsible for them. But for adults, heaven promises so much more: endless joy, rest from schedules and demands, no more disappointment or fear, and best of all, the opportunity to see God "up close and personal," the happily-ever-after ending that truly never ends.

I've started looking for ways to bring a bit of heaven into life here on earth. I want to cultivate a heavenly perspective unlike the old looking-over-my-shoulder-to-see-if-I'm-going-to-get-zapped-for-something-I-said-or-did mentality.

Several women I surveyed talked about how their attitudes toward the spiritual expectations they grew up with are changing:

One young woman says, "As a teen struggling with rebellion, I had many doubts. I felt that if I truly was a Christian, how could I think and feel as I did?"

Another says her biggest spiritual challenge is "living a life that is a relationship with God and not just *dos* and *don'ts*. The outward behavior is not that different, but the attitude and motivation are totally different."

Carol, a Christian psychologist, admits that she always felt inadequate, dissatisfied, even dwarfed by her accomplishments and duties. After struggling for years with perfectionism and her perceived obligation to "fix everybody," she says, "I am learning that when I stop trying too hard I can relax in His love and who He made me to be."

It's true that God has given us some absolutes to follow, but they're built on His fundamental loving care for us. We give children *dos* and *don'ts*, such as "Wash your hands after making mudpies if you want to eat lunch with us," and "Don't play tag in the middle of the freeway." Why? Because we want to spoil all their fun? No. Because we don't want them to digest bacteria with their bologna or to be trounced by the traffic.

Immaturity resents boundaries. Maturity respects them.

A Heavenly Friendship

God is eager to develop a maturing relationship with us that's saturated with His love. He is delighted when we come to Him for counsel rather than trying to prove we can make it on our own. He wants us to know that the rules He sets aren't designed to make us miserable. They are intended to save us from becoming smooshed critters on the freeway of life.

When our kids were little, sometimes we didn't have to punish them for their misdeeds. I would simply recite in sing-song fashion a phrase they soon dreaded hearing: "Sometimes when we're naughty, we wind up punishing ourselves."

To cite one of the less embarrassing examples, our youngest recalls a time, during our brief flirtation with cable television, when she sneaked out of bed to watch a forbidden scary TV show. Even her sister had warned her she would have bad dreams, but our little one convinced herself she could handle it. She did, indeed, learn that sometimes when we're naughty we wind up punishing ourselves—this time through nightmares aplenty.

Of course, along with that little saying, we also tried to remember to dispense hugs generously and tell our kids that their errant behavior in no way changed our love for them. It hasn't always been easy to move past our disappointment in some of their choices, especially during their "experimental" teen years. But having enjoyed God's unqualified love ourselves, we want to demonstrate that same love to them.

Most of us, I think, keenly feel our own shortcomings. What we sometimes forget is how much God loves us. We get tired of "battling the same sins over and over," as one woman told me, and we may feel that one of these days God is going to say,

"Enough is enough," and give up on us.

Yet repeatedly the Bible tells us about God's *unfailing love*. "'Though the mountains be shaken and the hills be removed, yet my unfailing love for you will not be shaken...' says the Lord, who has compassion on you" (Isaiah 54:10).

What a freeing concept! What security! And what a great motivation! We will still confess our sins, but we can say, "Satisfy us in the morning with your unfailing love," as Moses prays in Psalm 90, "that we may sing for joy and be glad all our days" (v. 14). It's easier to want to please someone we know won't give up on us.

But first we need to make sure that we have a personal relationship with God. He proved His unfailing love for us by sending His perfect Son, Jesus Christ, to suffer the punishment we deserve for our sins. He was the only sinless person ever to walk this earth, so He was the only one qualified to take the penalty for anyone else.

In His unfailing love, Jesus allowed Himself to be crucified to pay for the sins we have committed, the sins that keep us from having a relationship with God in the first place. "For the wages of sin is death," the Bible says, "but the gift of God is eternal life in Christ Jesus our Lord" (Romans 6:23). Then Jesus came back to life three days later to give us new life through Him.

If we accept His death as the payment for our sins and look to Him to guide our lives, we begin a lifelong *friendship* with Him (not a lifelong rule-keeping drive) here on earth that spills over into "forever" in heaven.

Raychelle, a young Minnesota mother, grew up chafing under the *dos* and *don'ts* of her family's religious teachings. Her parents raised their eleven children in what they felt was

"God's way," but Raychelle felt stifled by all the rules. Her parents' definition of living to please God "clashed with the sophisticated, successful, and self-reliant woman I had imagined to become," she says.

Her perspective changed a few years ago when she realized Christianity was a relationship with Jesus Christ, not a mammoth behavior checklist. As she began studying the Bible for herself, she found that some of her family's rules weren't even there. So she began sorting out what was biblical and what wasn't. "It was so freeing," she says.

For instance, she had been taught by word and example that being nice to people more or less meant doing anything anyone asked. As a result she couldn't turn anyone down and was perpetually overcommitted. "I would accept commitments," Raychelle says, "knowing I wouldn't follow through and knowing I would probably call and cancel later."

Her relationship with Christ, however, helped her see that Jesus said to let your *yes* be *yes* and your *no* be *no*. He gives us permission to say *no*—to protect us from getting conked on the head from trying to juggle too many hats at once.

Now, as the Lord shows Raychelle what is right, she does it out of love for Him. "How different that is!" she says.

What a heavenly perspective!

An Encouraging Legacy

When Judy Kendzora, a close friend of mine for more than twenty years, began leading women's Bible studies in our former church, the leaders asked her to fill out a questionnaire about what she had learned in her spiritual life. She summed it up in what she called Seven Lessons for Life:

1. God is good and all-wise. I can trust Him. He loves me and always deals with me out of love.

2. God doesn't owe me anything. All I have is by His grace. He doesn't owe me health, long life, or wealth. But I owe Him everything.

3. God's Word stands above my perceptions. His Word is true.

4. What goes on in the thought life determines attitudes. Philippians 4 teaches that we have a responsibility to think positively.

5. One must read the Bible daily to know God. It can't be done any other way. Obedient people get to know God, and you can't obey what you don't know.

6. The life standards laid down in the Bible are for my protection, not designed to deny me anything.

7. If I need it, God will take care of it.

A few days after she wrote these words, while driving home from teaching a Bible study about heaven, she was struck by a semi-truck and killed instantly—a hit-and-run collision. She went home to her *forever home* that she had just been telling others about.

I can't help but feel we'll enjoy heaven so much more if we spend time getting to know God now.

Strengthening Our Friendship With God

The women I surveyed offered various approaches to becoming better friends with God. Most said they read a few verses from the Bible (God's love letter to us), think about how that applies to their lives, and pray for their loved ones and personal concerns. Others use devotional books as well. Some sing songs of praise to the God they love.

I like to keep a notebook, writing out thoughts that come as I try to personalize what I hear God saying in the verses I read. I also talk to God on paper, so to speak, thanking Him for things He has done for me and working through concerns and difficulties as they arise.

Nearly all who responded to the survey admitted they struggle—as I do—to make time to visit with God regularly. It may help to picture ourselves sitting down with the Lord and sharing thoughts over a cup of coffee or a Coke as good friends often do.

But we need frequent exposure to Scripture in one form or another. God's Word aligns us with His way of thinking. It keeps us from being overwhelmed with today's crises that we'll forget tomorrow. It hits us over the head with reminders of stuff we already know but still need to hear from time to time:

We read the biographies of godly men and women in the Old Testament, and we learn that God is interested in the smallest details of our lives, that He's definitely the God of the second chance, and that He's able to forgive our mistakes, our blunders, and our outright rebellion—yet use us anyway.

We read the Psalms and we know it's OK to tell God when we're angry as well as when we're thrilled with who He is, what He has made, and what He's doing in our lives.

Proverbs reminds us how to get along with people, how to grow in integrity, and how to weave God's wisdom into our everyday decisions.

The prophecies excite us about being on the winning side.

The Gospels show us Jesus—our model for love in action.

We read the letters in the New Testament and are encouraged to strengthen our love relationship with the Lord, to keep our lives pure, to build up one another, and to press on.

When we go a step further and commit Scripture to memory, the Lord can bring His living words to our harried minds at the most opportune moments. Whatever time we can spend in His Word—however we occupy that time—strengthens our friendship with Him.

Even when we can't find a quiet moment to sit down and read a passage of Scripture, we can keep the communication lines open twenty-four hours a day to talk to the God we love. Even our intercession for others can be spur-of-the-moment prayer. I like to think of such situations as prayer triggers.

On my normal route to just about anywhere, I pass a street with the same name as a friend of our son's. This young man came to know Christ in middle school, got in with the wrong crowd for a while, and has recently become excited about his faith again! Seeing his name on that street sign triggers my mind to pray for his continued growth.

Newscasts of flooding in North Dakota became a trigger to pray for the people and churches in that area, that God would comfort them and supply their needs as they worked to clean up and rebuild. Because our daughter and son-in-law lived in Grand Forks for a while, our sensitivity had grown.

On the day we learned our daughter was pregnant with her first baby, our first grandchild, I bought a key chain with a little bean-filled elephant attached, and every time I looked at that little elephant, it triggered a prayer for Baby.

All sorts of things can become prayer triggers for a brief chat with God right on the spot.

Becoming More Alike

After more than two-and-a-half decades of marriage, it seems I'm always telling Steve, "I knew you were going to say that." And he has become quite proficient at finishing my sentences. It saves time, I guess. We've all seen married couples in their sixties and seventies who, after spending so many years together, begin to think, talk, act, and even look alike.

That's the way it is in our relationship with God, too. He can't change. We wouldn't want Him to. He is God. He is all we could ever want Him to be! But the more time we spend with Him, the more *we* begin to think, talk, and act like *Him*. The Bible says that when we act like God, the world around us will know God is behind it (see Matthew 5:16).

We may not see the results immediately—just as we don't see the results of exercise after the first two or three days. In fact, we can feel awkward at first, feeling the pain. But once we make them a habit, both kinds of exercise build us up.

Of course this friendship with God isn't an equal partnership. He's in charge. He is, in effect, the Boss. But we can be *friends* with the Boss (see John 15:14). He looks forward to our times together. In all our hectic schedules and many responsibilities, as we spend time getting to know Him, He gives us the resources to wear our numerous hats well.

He Loves Me. He Loves Me Not?

Many of us come to crisis points in our lives when God doesn't act as we expect Him to or He doesn't answer our prayers in the way we had hoped. Then doubt seeps into our minds.

At the age of nine Melanie learned she had diabetes. "The injections, the diet, and the awful urine tests" overwhelmed her as a child, she says. Family and church leaders told her she could be healed if she just had faith, and her "eager little spirit clung to this belief wholeheartedly," as she puts it. For years, ministers and church elders prayed over her often. She prayed constantly for healing, refusing to entertain the mere suggestion of doubt lest she negate the faith she had cultivated.

After seventeen years Melanie came to accept the fact that God's answer to her prayers was *no*. Her faith crumbled. For two years she didn't even consider herself a Christian.

"When God didn't do what I expected, I questioned His character, not my expectations," she admits. "I questioned His Word, not my interpretation of it. It was painful to abandon my dreams, but I had to let go of my conception of what God ought to do and how He ought to show His love. I had to let Him be Lord of my life and accept His answers."

Little by little, the Lord drew Melanie back. Most of all, she learned that "God is with us, supporting us and carrying us *through* life's difficulties, rather than rescuing us *from* life's difficulties."

Remember that little petal-pinching, sure-fire way to tell if the boy we had a crush on in sixth grade had any interest in us? I will admit to manipulating the test a bit by counting two petals as one or precounting the petals to assure the results. But we never have to manipulate the test with God. Every petal on every flower in all of creation is a He-loves-me petal. Not one says, "He loves me not."

Who—or what—can keep God from loving us? Nothing, the Bible says. "I am convinced that nothing can ever separate us from His love. Death can't, and life can't. The angels won't, and all the powers of hell itself cannot keep God's love away. Our fears for today, our worries about tomorrow ... nothing will ever be able to separate us from the love of God demonstrated by our Lord Jesus Christ when he died for us" (Romans 8:38-39, LB).

When I was a child I learned a Bible verse for each letter of the alphabet. The *D* verse, "Draw nigh to God, and he will draw nigh to you" (James 4:8, KJV) deeply embedded itself in my memory. Though I didn't fully understand it then, it proved itself true over and over. No matter how much we may have doubted or how far we may have strayed from our commitment to Him, the Lord is eager to welcome us back as friends.

Our hat as a friend of God, of course, isn't *actually* a halo, indicating some superior level of perfection. Far from it. We're all fellow strugglers. We rely on our Creator to help us understand how we are made and to give us the power to think and act in ways that please Him.

A single friend of mine says, "One of the blessings of being alone is that [often] I can have uninterrupted time with God—sometimes talking, sometimes thinking, sometimes asking, sometimes just the quietness of dealing with a lump in my throat, knowing He cares."

Even those of us who have family around live a good percentage of our lives inside our thoughts. We can direct those thoughts heavenward, developing a heavenly perspective on every detail of our day. "Set your minds on things above, not on earthly things," God says. "For ... your life is now hidden with Christ in God" (Colossians 3:2-3).

It is such a privilege to know God personally through His Son, Jesus Christ. And when we wear the friend-of-God hat well, all our other hats fit much better!

My Sister, My Friend?

Everything in the spiritual realm, it seems, is built on relationships—with God and with one another. How's your friend-to-friend or sisterhood hat? This one gets battered around and wrinkled and sat upon more often than we'd like to admit.

As friends and children of God, we women who follow Him are sisters. What a great model—if you focus on caring, encouraging adult sister relationships rather than those hair pulling, second-guessing, why-do-Mom-and-Dad-like-you-best? tattle-tale days of childhood.

Or maybe that's why we have trouble with some of our female friendships. Maybe we haven't completely outgrown those relating habits of playground days.

My niece Kim points out that women tend to look for hidden meanings in what we say to each other. "What did she mean by that?" could be our gender's national anthem, I think. Kim and my daughter spent most of their childhood as best friends and worst enemies simultaneously. Whenever they were together or talking on the phone, they would invariably end up reading ulterior motives and unspoken jabs into everything—even silence.

A former boss of mine, Carol, tells about a time when her answering machine decided to quit working but didn't have the courtesy to let her know. A friend in great distress left a message on the machine, asking Carol to call her as soon as she got in. Carol never received the message. After several days without a return call, the friend convinced herself that Carol didn't care about her at all.

Unfortunately, our what-did-she-mean-by-that? second-guessing often turns into gossip or slander when we tell others what-we-*think*-she-meant-by-that.

Recently a young woman related a hurtful conversation to me. Her mother-in-law had made a remark, which the younger woman interpreted as a put-down. I took up my young friend's cause. "I can't believe she was that rude," I comforted. We talked about how difficult it was to forgive sometimes, and she assured me she had forgiven her mother-in-law. But I'm ashamed to admit I never said, "Maybe she didn't mean it that way."

Oh, how foreign to what God intended in mature sister relationships! In a passage focusing on the relationships of Christian women, the Bible cites several important character qualities God wants us to nurture—some relating to wives and moms, but three that relate to all of us: self-control, kindness, and purity (see Titus 2:3–5).

A painter was painting the lunchroom where three office workers were drinking coffee and discussing a fourth woman who had been brought in to handle a new project. The three didn't like her management style, and as their conversation continued, as often happens, their words became more and more brutal. The painter kept working, unable to avoid eavesdropping. But then the coffee drinkers began attacking the other woman's character. He could keep silent no more. "Excuse me," he said. "I'm going to have to ask you to stop. That woman you're talking about is my daughter."

My mom used to give us three rules to guard our conversations:

1. Is it true?

2. Is it nice?

3. Is it necessary?

We can better encourage each other if we use a little *self-control* in evaluating what others say and *purify* our thoughts by not allowing ourselves to think *unkindly* of another woman because of something we *think* she meant. We can better build each other up if we don't ruin another's reputation by passing along this secondhand second-guessing. When those thoughts come, we can "take captive every thought to make it obedient to Christ" (2 Corinthians 10:5).

Here are some things we can focus on when we're trying to lasso those runaway thoughts:

1. Most of what another person says to us is not malicious.

2. Reading malicious intent into her comments deafens me to the good things she says to and about me in the future. It also erects a barrier between us. I don't want to build walls between my sisters and me. I want to build bridges.

3. Deciding something she said was malicious tears her down in my eyes. If I pass along my suspicions, all who hear me will think less of her from now on.

We can't afford to become demolition experts. We need each other too much to be tearing each other down.

Relating and Nurturing—By Design

Our relational nature, as women, uniquely qualifies us to build one another up instead of tearing each other down. "Therefore encourage one another and build each other up," says the apostle Paul (1 Thessalonians 5:11).

The sister bond we have in Jesus Christ and the empathy He can give us for one another helps us cheer each other on in our often discouraging world of far-too-many hats.

Shelly tells a story about her mom's often uninhibited methods of encouraging her. While in high school Shelly tried out for a select band, which would travel to Europe in the spring. Her mom promised to pray for her and was eager to hear the results. But Shelly wouldn't have time to call home between the time she found out and the time she had to march in the football game that evening. So they devised a sign. When the band marched into the stadium, Shelly would flash a thumbs-up sign if she had been chosen for the honors band.

That evening as the uniformed band members marched rigidly onto the floodlight-drenched football field, Shelly looked up and saw her mom high in the bleachers with a pair of binoculars glued to her eyes. Shelly raised her thumb in triumph. Immediately her mom jumped up and, much to the bewilderment of the quiet fans around her, hollered, "Yea!" at the top of her lungs. The last thing Shelly saw, as she turned her attention back to the drum major, was her father cowering behind his hands in embarrassment.

We all need our own personal cheerleaders—sisters who will *cheer us on* when we succeed and *cheer us up* when we're discouraged. Unfortunately, juggling our many hats keeps us so busy we often don't notice each other's needs or take the time to encourage.

Remember Judith Viorst's children's book *Alexander and the Terrible, Horrible, No Good, Very Bad Day?* I love that title! Most of us have been there. But it's amazing how a little sensitivity can turn a terrible, horrible, no good, very bad day into a wonderful, fabulous, so good, very great one! Or at least one we can get through.

Several years ago, during a particularly long, gray, dreary

Minnesota winter that magnified my own personal difficulties, my friend Sharon brought me a bouquet of flowers in a ribbon-tied sixteen-ounce Coke bottle. (She knows my preferred brand of caffeine intake.) The attached card read: "Yes, Joyce, there is a springtime!" I've kept that little card and I use it as a bookmark. Each time I see it, it reminds me that no matter how gray and discouraging the circumstances, I have a God who brings spring after winter, and I have sisters who care about me. "One kind word," says a Japanese proverb, "can warm up three winter months."

Sensitivity is one of our strong points as women. Sometimes we view it as a negative trait, loathing our tendency to be easily hurt. But its flip side allows us to feel what another is going through and do what we can to help.

If we'll raise our sensitivity antennae, we can show that we care in many different ways:

1. *Passing notes.* Remember how we used to pass notes in school? If yours were like my friends' and mine, the subject matter usually focused on how interested the new guy was when he smiled at us or who was whose best friend. But maybe, as adult sisters who need encouragement from one another, we can revive that old note-passing practice for more noble purposes.

The note doesn't have to be long, even five or six words. You can send it through the mail, slip it under her door, or hand it to her between church services. But an "I'm thinking about you" or "I'm praying for you this week" can calm an office manager going into a budget meeting, help a new mom feel she's not alone as she changes the third dirty diaper of the morning, or fortify a college student facing an exam.

When we see someone accomplish something important to her, we can encourage with a note or homemade congratulations card. When we have been helped by something another woman said or did or by some music or drama presentation at our church, we can send a note or call to say thanks. We often forget how encouraging a simple thank you can be until we're the ones who hear it.

As more and more people are zipping onto the Information Superhighway "on ramp," e-mail can be a fun—and inexpensive—way to encourage one another (once you've drained your checkbook for the computer in the first place).

A small church in the St. Louis area has initiated what they call D-Mail—an opportunity to share gleanings from their devotional times (and prayer requests) with each other via the Internet. This has been an especially important link for their college students hundreds of miles away.

Several writer friends and I keep each other updated on projects and activities via e-mail so we know how to pray for each other. It's not as permanent as letters, but it's more immediate. And it's so exciting to share in each other's accomplishments this way!

Don't forget to pass along secondhand compliments, too. If you hear someone praising an acquaintance of yours, let her know. One of my friends makes a habit of this, believing that secondhand compliments mean even more because they're not empty flattery.

2. *Touch.* It's amazing how much a touch on the shoulder, the grasp of a hand, or a brief hug can help us connect with one another. Loving, appropriate touch says, "I care about you. We have an important bond. We're in this together."

I'll never forget the day I learned my friend Judy had died in a hit-and-run crash. Judy and I worked in the same office building along with our mutual friend Debbie. After we got to work and heard the news, Debbie met me in the lunchroom at break time, and we consoled each other with hugs and tears. Then Debbie clasped my hand and held it tightly for several minutes as together we grieved. The rest of the day the sweet vanilla aroma of her hand lotion remained on my hands, too. Although I had to go on with my work, that lingering fragrance helped me know I was not alone in my sorrow.

3. *Praying for one another.* It's so great to know that as followers of Christ, we sisters can talk to our Father about anything—especially when we face circumstances totally out of our hands. I am so grateful for my prayer partner, Bonnie. She and I get together weekly to talk over our concerns and pray. We pray for personal needs as well as the needs of our families and our church. And we've seen God answer in some spectacular ways—everything from last-minute cancellations that allowed me to get in earlier for a much-needed doctor's appointment to working out carpool arrangements for Bonnie.

Have you ever tried praying together over the phone? The first time someone suggested it, I felt awkward. But what a great encouragement it is to discuss a problem with someone on the phone and have her say, "Let's pray about it right now."

For several months last year, another friend and I were prayer partners. We didn't know each other well when we started meeting together, but we soon discovered that we had some of the same health struggles and family concerns. So we began viewing our own "troubles" as triggers to pray for the other. For example, while swallowing medication for my own tendinitis flare-ups, I'd pray for my friend's struggle with similar pain. That's one way to pray continually, as the Bible reminds us (see 1 Thessalonians 5:17).

4. *Family get-togethers.* After my mother-in-law died a few years ago, my husband's siblings, who lived in three states and seldom saw each other, wanted to stay in touch better. Now each autumn they rent an entire Bed & Breakfast for a weekend and play games, look at photo albums, and tell each other's kids all the crazy stunts they used to pull. It's a time of fun and mutual encouragement.

As followers of Christ, we sisters need our family get-togethers, too. Our Sunday worship services, women's Bible studies, and other church activities are great opportunities to learn about each other's needs and to encourage one another.

But sometimes we're not very honest with each other. I know that in our society when someone says, "How are you?" convention dictates a Pollyannish "Fine" even if we spent all night running to fetch enough buckets to catch the twenty-two leaks in our roof.

If we would admit when we've had a lousy week or an unspeakable run-in with our unreasonable boss, we wouldn't experience this feeling that everybody's got it together but us. Sometimes those who seem to have it together are most in need of our prayer and encouragement.

"Psst! Pass It On ..."

Having grown up in a fairly small church, there are a few things I have missed since becoming part of a larger congregation. One is the cross-generational camaraderie. Many big churches tend to compartmentalize people by age group. Adult Sunday school classes can be divided into career-starting lights of the world, about-to-become-one-in-Jesus believers, honeymooners-in-Christ forever, victorious-though-sleep-deprived-new-parent fellowshipers, overcoming-mid-life-crisis encouragers, all the way up through seasoned saints, a euphemism for those we expect to meet their Maker any day.

But in our efforts to be with people of like interests and similar stages of life, we often lose something—that intergenerational sharing of wisdom and encouragement. Older women can be encouraged by the enthusiasm and vision of younger women, and younger women can learn from the wisdom and experience of older women. (And there is no way you're going to get me to draw that nebulous line between the two.) Both older and younger can build each other up through mutual encouragement. My grandmother was just such an encourager.

When I was in high school, my mom worked outside the home, but often when I came home from school, my grandmother would have a cup of tea and a well-tuned ear ready, waiting for me to pour out the ups and downs of my day. Sometimes she would just listen. Other times she would tell me things she had learned about handling similar circumstances. Often she would give me a verse of Scripture to think about. How grateful I am for her encouragement.

My sister Jan remembers the night she came home after quitting nurses' training. She felt like a failure. Not wanting to see or talk to anyone, she retreated to her basement bedroom. After the house was dark and quiet, she ventured upstairs to the bathroom, but as she opened the door to the main floor, she felt a pair of loving arms wrap around her. "You know we still love you, don't you?" our grandmother said.

"God used Grandma's arms to hug me," Jan says. Grandma had stepped in as her best cheerleader. "There were times that only she could reach through my confusion and love my innermost self."

Missy feels the same way about the grandmas and great-grandmas that participate in the Bible study she goes to. "They're so patient and gentle, and I've learned so much from them," she says.

I felt the same way about a group of women I used to meet with once a month to work on baby layettes and quilts for missionaries. I was a young mom, and many of them were old enough to be my mother, but I learned a lot about being a good wife and mother and woman of God through our conversations as we worked together and laughed together.

Sensitivity—It's a Good Thing!

"Likewise, teach the older women to be reverent in the way they live, not to be slanderers or addicted to much wine, but to teach what is good," wrote Paul to a church leader named Titus. "Then they can train the younger women to love their husbands and children, to be self-controlled and pure, to be busy at home, to be kind, and to be subject to their husbands, so that no one will malign the word of God" (Titus 2:3-5).

Think of it! How we relate to each other, how we learn from each other, and how we relate in our families impact those who don't know the Lord Jesus Christ. If we don't learn from each other how to respond to life's stresses in a godly way, those who don't know Christ will have reason to point and say,

"What good is it to follow the ways of what they call the Word of God?"

When we hang around with only people of our own age group, we can sometimes lose perspective. Our get-togethers can become gripe sessions which vent our frustrations but don't build each other up. Younger moms need older moms to provide perspective and to act as cheerleaders who can say, "You're gonna make it! You're not going to die of dishpan hands or diaper changing or Sesame Street conversations."

It can be awkward for an older woman to approach a young mom and say, "I've noticed you need help loving your husband and children." So, young mothers, if no one comes up to you and offers, find a godly older woman whom you admire, and ask if you can get together with her periodically—even just to talk. Most often, I think you'll find she would be honored.

Younger singles also need older women to remind them that it's worth it to follow God's ways in personal purity or doing business or relating to their roommates. Older women need younger women, to unjade their outlook and to spread contagious enthusiasm and dream new dreams. Whether we're in small churches or large ones, we need to find ways to come alongside and give each other the courage to wear our many hats well.

As sisters,

- We can develop a sensitivity to others' gifts, talents, and accomplishments—and encourage.
- We can develop a sensitivity to others' areas of discouragement and weakness—and encourage.
- We can develop a sensitivity to ways of showing we care—and encourage.

It's best to take a few seconds or minutes and encourage at the moment we think of it. If we put it off, we'll start thinking it will take longer than it will, and we probably won't do it at all. Then both the giver and the recipient will get gypped, to borrow an expression from our playground days. So let's "encourage one another daily, as long as it is called Today" (Hebrews 3:13), to help each other balance that ever-increasingly heavy load of hats on our heads.

There's one more way we can encourage one another, but that requires plopping yet another hat on our heads. One we sometimes wear without even noticing....

Study Questions

1. Read 1 John 3:1-5, Isaiah 54:10, Psalm 90:14, and Romans 8:38-39 (read this last passage in *The Living Bible* if possible). How do we know that all God's commandments to us are in our best interest? Some people think they have done something so terrible that God has given up on them. From these verses, how do we know that God never gives up on us?

2. Read John 3:16, Romans 6:23, John 1:12, and Ephesians 2:8-9. How can a person have a personal relationship with Jesus Christ?

3. Read John 15:14-15. Those who put their trust in Jesus Christ are not only His servants but what? How do we demonstrate that?

4. Read James 4:8. How can we become closer to God? Practically speaking, what does that entail?

5. Read Colossians 3:2-3. What can we do in our minds to avoid getting bogged down with all our many responsibilities as women?

6. Read 1 Thessalonians 5:11,14-18; Hebrews 3:13; and Titus 2:3-5. How can putting these things into practice help us juggle our many hats better?

7. Read James 5:16. What is the greatest thing we can do for one another?

SEVEN

Why Does My Maid's Cap Keep Slipping?

~

My Role as Servant of All

I think that God gives us a special privilege to be a servant ... we don't even have to look for places to serve. It is our environment, where we live.

—Helene Zedicher
Her hats include those of a retired
school food service cashier, wife of a
retired draftsman, mother of five
grown children and grandmother
of nine.

We ordered take-out Chinese. The little strip of paper in my husband's fortune cookie said, "You will be surrounded by luxury." Mine said, "It's always a good time to lend a helping hand."

Is that fair? He gets luxury and I get *servanthood*?

Of course it's just a fortune cookie, but why do we hate the idea of "serving" so much?

Perhaps in our heads we have visions of Disney's soot-covered Cinderella scrubbing the floors on her pruney hands and knees while her two ugly stepsisters sit around on their bustles telling her she's not doing it right.

Perhaps a poor attitude toward the chores parents expected us to do in our childhood made us long for the day we'd be in charge and wouldn't feel we existed only to be someone's galley slaves.

Perhaps the loudest voices of the past thirty years or so have convinced us that the word *servanthood*—for our gender—is profanity.

But, as usual, our inward feelings and society's outcries are not always God's ways. We need to make sense of all our hat shuffling. But the answer isn't to stew over male-female injustices or people's unrealistic expectations. I do find it interesting that "more freedoms" for women seem to have given us more hats to juggle rather than fewer. But I believe the key to hat management is to develop the loving, nurturing, intuitive servant heart God created within us. A servant heart provides a proper perspective on our own situation and helps us realize our God-given *inter*dependence as women.

God says, "Serve one another by love" (Galatians 5:13). Serving one another—and allowing others to serve us—as God intended, lightens the load for each of us. Loving interdependence—if we'll open ourselves to it—helps us balance our precarious pile of hats.

Corrective Lenses for Nearsightedness

What gets in the way of this loving, interdependent servant spirit? Something I call the Mr. Magoo Syndrome. Perhaps you remember TV's lovable nearsighted cartoon character who bumped into one crisis after another.

A lot of elements go into the Mr. Magoo Syndrome: independence, selfishness and self-centeredness (they're not the same), pride, lack of faith, worry, and more.

Suzanne, a Texas woman, believes in the importance of being a joyful servant, but, she says, "My selfish nature gets in the way and sometimes I feel I am being taken advantage of or that I don't have anyone serving me."

It's human nature to want to be the one in the limelight, to want to be the guest once in a while instead of always being the one doing the work or at least to get credit when we've slaved for others. But that's our human, sinful nature. When we have accepted Christ as our Savior and Master, His Holy Spirit lives within us and gives us another nature that is more powerful (and more noble) than our human nature—if we choose to yield to it.

Suzanne began to realize that it's not true that no one is serving her. "Jesus is serving me," she says. "He died for me and rose again for me. He carries away all my sin. His loving arms hold me up when I am tired. He comforts me when I'm sad. He floods me with peace when I am anxious."

Our Lord Jesus Christ is the ultimate example of service. He said He didn't come to be served (even though He, as truly God and truly man, had every right to be). Instead He came to serve—to serve *us* (see Matthew 20:28).

He didn't insist on His "rights" as we are so often prone to do. The apostle Paul cites Christ's attitude as our model: "Each of you should look not only to your own interests, but also to the interests of others. Your attitude should be the same as that of Christ Jesus...taking the very nature of a servant" (Philippians 2:4-7).

Years ago someone told me that we would be surprised at

how much God could accomplish in this world if we didn't care who got the credit for it. That has been a tremendous encouragement to me. It's a model of servanthood.

Amy, a young Iowa mom, grew up learning to fend for herself. She learned that if you want things done, "you do it yourself." But as her relationship with God has matured, He has helped her become more of a servant for Him. "Therefore I am able to be a servant for my husband, kids, and other family members," she says. "If I didn't want to serve the Lord, I don't think I could serve others."

If we think about His goodness to us, our gratitude will spill over into servanthood toward those around us, which, in turn, is service for Him.

A verse I memorized in adolescence has become a life motto for me. I've even taped it to my computer monitor: "Only fear the Lord and serve Him in truth with all your heart; for consider what great things He has done for you" (1 Samuel 12:24, NASB). That's what Suzanne was talking about. I like the way she put it: "His loving arms hold me up when I am tired. He comforts me when I'm sad. He floods me with peace when I am anxious." All this on top of the greatest gift anyone could receive: giving His life to pay for our sins.

Magoo Transformed

Our natural nearsighted perspective chafes under other people's demands. But with Christ's model as our corrective lenses, we can see our hats as opportunities to serve Him. Then we can tap into those nurturing, relational qualities He put within us to help us serve lovingly and joyfully. We can do it all as though we were doing it for Him directly. Jesus said, "I tell you the truth, whatever you did for one of the least of these brothers of mine, you did for me" (Matthew 25:40).

Some time ago I was organizing a special tea for an organization I belong to, and, as usual, my plans became more and more grandiose until they got out of hand. I found myself running all over town to borrow teapots and teacups to make this a memorable evening. Because some of the borrowed items had been in storage, they needed to be washed before I took them to the event.

My husband had already lovingly washed the teacups from my own collection that had been attracting dust as they sat on their display shelf. (I've learned a lot about servanthood from him.) But as I leaned over the sudsy sink, not trusting these borrowed items to our not-so-trusty automatic dishwasher, my feet throbbed and back ached.

My thoughts zeroed in on me. I wondered if anyone would appreciate all the work I had put into this occasion. I felt "put upon," though I had to admit I had put all this upon myself and hadn't asked for much help.

Then I started thinking about what an opportunity this was going to be to serve—not just those who were coming to the tea but Christ Himself. God says, "Whatever you do, whether in word or deed, do it all in the name of the Lord Jesus, giving thanks to God the Father through him" (Colossians 3:17).

Before long I was humming the tune to a little praise song called "I Love You, Lord," and new words attached themselves to the tune in my mind:

I love You, Lord, and I give my hands
to serve You, Lord. It's my joy right now.
Be pleased, dear Lord, with what You see,
May it be a sweet, sweet sight in Your eyes.

It doesn't rhyme, but as I sang this little bit of praise over and over, I can truthfully say my attitude changed to one of great delight.

I wish I could say I always respond this way, but more often than I'd like to admit, I've stewed in the mess of my own concoction far too long. How much better it was to delight in this opportunity to serve Christ with soapsuds and a towel.

Oddly enough, those were the two items Jesus used to model servanthood to us. Remember how Jesus got up after a meal He had enjoyed with His disciples and washed their feet and dried them with a towel? (see John 13).

Linda, a pastor's wife, says that when her husband graduated from seminary, the school's president spoke about servanthood and gave all the graduates a tiny square of towel to keep in their wallets. That visual reminder to keep a servant's heart has stuck with Linda and her husband for years. But it's not just for pastors and their wives. It's for all of us.

Sometimes the "towel" looks more like a cleaning rag. My sister Jeanne remembers an incident when all her kids were still home. One day, as she was down on the floor "hugging and scrubbing the potty," as she puts it, she surprised herself as she began singing a song our kids learned when they were little: "Love Is Something You Do."

Servanthood and love cling together.

Strengthening Our Farsightedness

Servanthood and encouragement also intertwine beautifully. What an encouragement it is when another person pays attention to us—when someone *notices* we're struggling or are about to trip over the hats that are falling because they're piled too high, when someone picks up one or two of those hats and carries them for us for a little while.

Thoughtful, practical acts of kindness show off interdependence at its finest.

At our newly planted but fast-growing church we have a motto: "With open hands, receiving from God all He wants to give us and with open hands giving it away, believing we can't outgive God." I like that! The apostle Paul wrote, "Therefore, as we have opportunity, let us do good to all people, especially to those who belong to the family of believers" (Galatians 6:10).

My friend Joyce Young already had three children when she became pregnant with twins. Though traditionally showers are given for first babies only, the women in her church "doused her well," supplying the additional needs of two babies at once. "Two of the women gave me a card that said they would baby-sit for our five kids so that my husband and I could go out to dinner when I felt recuperated," she says.

"The night arrived, and we were excited just to be able to get out for an evening alone, knowing our kids would be cared for by two capable and loving friends." As Joyce and her husband left the house, one of the women handed her a card and said, "Open this when you get in your car." Inside was $25 cash to be used for their dinner. "Wow!" Joyce says. "Did these ladies know what we needed or what? That has to be one of the best gifts we have ever received."

We are sisters. We are family. We take care of each other. *And we need to let each other know if we need help.*

An Extra Pair of Hands

I once heard comedian David Brenner reminisce about some of the things his mother said to him over and over when he was growing up. The one he remembered most was, "I only have two hands." Brenner said, "I hated to see what other people's mothers looked like."

There are days, however, when we wish we had an extra pair of hands to accomplish all the chores our many hats require of us.

Remember how in the "olden days" a relative might travel many miles to help a new mother for a few weeks when a baby was born? I appreciated my cousins who helped me when some of our kids were born. (I guess that positions me in the "olden days" category, doesn't it?) Having an extra pair of hands—whether this is baby number one, two, five, or eight—encourages a new mom so much. But we can help with loving hands in other areas as well.

One woman found herself in the hospital days before she planned to entertain out-of-town guests for a week. Confined to bed, she fretted about the last-minute cleaning that wouldn't get done before her guests arrived. A friend, remembering where the extra house key was hidden, secretly let herself in and played Ms. Clean in the kitchen and bathrooms. It didn't take long to spiff up the place, but both friends felt better when the guests arrived.

A lot of mothers are discovering the near miracle of baby-sitting co-ops. One mom I know takes care of her friends' kids one day a week, and the friend reciprocates, so each mother gets one day completely to herself.

In her highly practical book, *No More Lone Ranger Moms,* author Donna Partow outlines a number of other ways women can "circle the wagons" (to use her phrase borrowed from our pioneer grandmothers) and help each other. Suggestions range from business support networks to supervised playgroups to clothing exchanges to food co-ops. Her chapter on how to work well with different personality types is alone worth the price of the book. But above all, what she's calling for is a new women's movement. "Not for independence," she writes, "but for interdependence. Not one born of anger toward men, but of love for one another. Not one to demand our rights, but to own up to our responsibility to help each other along this incredibly difficult journey."[1]

Several years ago some friends of ours experienced a house fire in the middle of the night. They escaped with little injury, but the house and most of their possessions were destroyed. Another couple in their church salvaged a few things and spent hours cleaning them up. I'll never forget our friends' faces as they told us about this fellow who spent hours scrubbing a cherished Precious Moments figurine with a toothbrush until all the grimy, black soot came out of every little crevice. That's loving, encouraging servanthood.

The more we serve one another in love (see Galatians 5:13) the easier our loads become. But it takes a certain amount of chutzpah to step out of our four walls and get involved in other people's lives—and to let them get close to us.

Fast Food Redefined

Some churches still practice another bit of thoughtfulness by providing meals when women are hospitalized, bedridden at home, have new babies, or experience a death in the family. When I was in and out of the hospital for nearly a month with pancreatitis several years ago, the women in our adult Sunday school class took turns bringing entire meals every night. I could keep very little food down at the time, but at least I knew my family wouldn't be begging food door-to-door.

Kenda, a woman in our Bible study group, was touched deeply by the sorrow of a new couple in our church who had lost a baby only a few days after birth. When Kenda passed around a sign-up sheet for women to provide food, she had enough offers for three weeks. That's servanthood!

But this practice need not be limited to times of sickness, or new babies, or a death in the family.

Cindy, a mother of grade-schoolers and teenagers, works part-time. One summer morning as she was leaving to chauffeur her kids to their activities, do errands, and go to work, a neighbor met her outside. "How's your day?" the neighbor asked.

"Terrible," Cindy said. Feeling defeated by her monstrous schedule before the day even began, she mentioned a few of the many things she had to do.

"Why don't you let me bring dinner over tonight?" the neighbor offered.

Cindy could hardly refuse. When she returned from work and errands that afternoon, she found a casserole, salad, and dessert waiting in her refrigerator.

If we do the cooking in our home—or assist our husbands

in the task—as long as we're preparing a meal, it doesn't take that much to double our recipes and share with someone else. But what a gift for the person on the receiving end!

I must admit that when I first heard this story, my first two (nearsighted) reactions were "How come nobody offers me meals when I've got a lot to do?" and "I think I need to move into *that* neighborhood." Then, of course, the Lord needled me with "When was the last time you offered that kind of help?"

Our lives are full of give-and-take. And we need to do both graciously. But strengthening our farsightedness instead of stumbling around in our nearsightedness brings us a little closer to the model of Christ.

Hospitality "Sweet"

I'm grateful for my grandmother, mother, aunts, and older sister who have modeled hospitality for me. Their homes were open to our friends, family, visiting missionaries, or anyone in need. What a rich life I've had, meeting so many diverse people, often seeing them transformed as they relaxed in a warm, inviting home.

My sister Jeanne practices some of the most farsighted hospitality I've ever seen. Besides opening her home to friends, relatives, and friends of relatives, she hosts weekly Bible studies and other gatherings in her home. Numerous young people of various ethnic backgrounds have lived with Jeanne's family for weeks, months, even more than a year at a time.

Perhaps one of her most unusual farsighted acts of service is her annual Halloween outreach. Every year she sets up a table in her front yard to serve donuts and hot cider to parents of the one-night Batmen and Beauties and Beasts. On what is usually a chilly night in Minnesota, parents often welcome a hot drink and a warm conversation. Her cider and donuts have become legendary in her neighborhood, and she often uses the opportunity to pass along a word about Christ or a copy of *Pursuit*, an attractive magazine designed to tell non-Christians how they can have a personal relationship with Jesus Christ.[2]

Jeanne's farsighted hospitality even reaches out hundreds of miles from home. Once, while visiting a friend in Iowa, her hostess was gone for the morning and Jeanne noticed some new neighbors moving in. She popped into her car and bought a rose to take to them. Later she appeared on their doorstep with a basket containing breakfast cereal, milk, and pretty, matching disposable plates, bowls, cups, and plasticware.

A servant heart has eyes that look for the most practical ways to help—no matter how trivial or awkward they may seem.

Nothing Too Small

I like the little Southern or country expression—*spelling one another*. People take turns staying with someone or helping "for a spell." We, as women, need to spell one another with encouragement through the tough times so we don't end up exhausted and desperate.

When my mother-in-law was dying of lung cancer, she wanted to remain at home rather than accumulate hospital bills. Her greatest fear, however, was being alone through the night. Local hospice care provided limited help, so women from her small town and her local church took turns "sleeping over." Perhaps we might think about doing the same for a newly widowed or newly divorced woman—now alone for the first time in years, perhaps decades.

Single moms, too, often struggle greatly with their increased number of hats and often diminished resources. Jean Bracken, a former coworker of mine, says that when her children were small, a single mother in her neighborhood was struggling financially, so Jean took care of her boys without charging her. "Many nights she had dinner with us," Jean says, "so she did not have to prepare a meal when she went home."

What a beautiful example of "Carry each other's burdens, and in this way you will fulfill the law of Christ" (Galatians 6:2)!

Tammy, the director of a North Carolina crisis pregnancy center, was impressed with a new young doctor in town who offered to do some volunteer work there. Excited about the possibility of a doctor on the volunteer staff, Tammy envisioned opening a clinic and expanding services. "Actually," the doctor responded, "I see myself fitting in by folding newsletters or something like that."

That's humility, the hallmark of a servant. Jesus said, "If anyone wants to be first, he must be the very last, and the servant of all" (Mark 9:35).

Passing the Baton

When do we begin teaching the next generation about servanthood? When we encourage younger friends to use their talents to help another person in need, we're doing it. When our children see us joyfully serving others, we're doing it. When we help our children develop their own areas of service, we're doing it, too.

A woman I know spends several hours a week reading to the elderly. Her daughter caught the bug, too. I don't know many high school kids who would take time out of their frenetic schedules of school, job, and social activities to do something that to them might seem trivial. But this teenager saw the joy in her mom's life as she modeled serving others, and the daughter got hooked on servanthood, too.

I'll never forget Hazel Hawkins, a woman in my home church in St. Louis. When I was about twelve, she invited a handful of girls my age to work together on scrapbooks that she took to nursing homes and sent to missionaries. On each page we pasted a beautiful scenic wall calendar picture and an appropriate Scripture verse or two cut out of old Bibles. It was fun to work together on the projects and to hear the delight of those who received them. I have her to thank for another fun model of a farsighted servant spirit. (Come to think of it, I also have her to thank for the fact that to this day I cannot throw away any wall calendars.)

But she worked *with* us. That's what I remember most. Intergenerational working together.

I've been in groups with older members who said (or implied), "We've served our time. We've done our part. Now it's your turn." And they simply turned over the organizational and planning aspects to the younger members with little or no sharing of experience-born wisdom. That type of attitude frustrates incoming leadership. Ironically, the "outgoing" leaders often then complain when new "servants" don't do things "the way they've always been done."

Another sports analogy may help here. I love the double meaning in the term *human race*. Sometimes life seems like a marathon requiring incredible perseverance. Sometimes we feel we need to be hurdlers to make it through the living room without tripping over our preschoolers' toys. Sometimes our days seem like a series of sprints as we try to keep up with adolescents or adolescent-acting bosses. But I think one of the most important metaphors for the human race is the relay.

My kids all ran track in high school, and they each ran relays from time to time. Their workouts included practicing baton passes from one runner to the next—over and over again. The exchange only takes a moment, but we watched many meets in which the relay was won or lost on the strength, precision, and smoothness of the passing of the baton.

While baton passing on a track oval is brief, in real life it often takes months, perhaps years. That's what families are about. That's what intergenerational working together as servants is about.

For a time both hands need to grasp the baton. As previous leaders work patiently with new ones—with a servant heart— all those new tasks seem less overwhelming. This is even true in teaching children chores. Unfortunately, many of us over-schedule ourselves so much that by the time our term is up, we're exhausted. We don't want to deal with those headaches anymore. But bringing new leaders in sooner for a little baton-passing practice lightens each person's load, prepares new officers for their tasks, and creates a smoother transition.

The other side of this coin, of course, is the runner who won't let go of the baton. This woman fears giving up leadership because the next person might not do things the way she thinks they should be done. She usually falls prey to burnout or becomes bitter because others don't do their part.

God, in His usual loving way, has put us in families and in local churches and in communities to help one another—to serve one another. If we're having difficulty managing all our hats, we may not be taking advantage of the give-and-take He desires for us. We may be letting pride obscure our vision of God working through others. We may be holding on to the baton longer than we should or acting like the Lone Ranger. But, as someone has said, "Even the Lone Ranger had Tonto."

Fringe Benefits

God has promised rewards to His faithful servants. And I must admit that part of my motivation in servanthood is to someday hear Him say, "Well done, *good and faithful* servant." With my competitive nature, I can't deny I'm looking forward to the rewards He has promised to those who serve Him well.

I've heard some people say that if you receive rewards on earth for your service, you won't receive any rewards in heaven. I don't think that's what the Bible teaches. In Matthew 6:1, Jesus says, "Be careful not to do your 'acts of righteousness' before men, *to be seen by them.* If you do, you will have no reward from your Father in heaven" (emphasis mine). I believe Jesus was talking about motivation here.

In other words, don't do "servant stuff" so that people will think you are wonderful or spiritual or even a great servant. If that's your *motivation*, then that's your reward. But just because someone thanks you or compliments you or gives you a distinguished service award doesn't necessarily mean that you won't receive a reward from God as well. If you acted out of love for God and care for the other person, the heavenly reward awaits.

Of course if you only worked hard to beat out your lifelong rival for "The Most Spiritual Christian of the Year Award," you might want to polish your plaque often—'cause that's all you're gonna get!

A servant spirit bears the burdens of others—not to impress but out of love for Christ. "For consider what great things He has done for you" (1 Samuel 12:24, NASB).

If you're not sure how pure your motives are, try a little anonymous servanthood. Giving isn't a spectator sport, anyway! Don't even tell a friend or your husband what you've done. It's great fun—especially if you can observe the recipient's reaction.

Psychologist Carol Travilla says, "I am the Lord's freelance servant committed to His training and consulting." As a freelance writer, I like that picture. Freelancers work for many organizations and individuals, doing whatever work is needed. Sometimes they work on assignment (when someone asks for help). Sometimes they generate their own ideas (offering their service to anyone who might be able to use it).

Whatever we do, the Bible says, we are to work at it with all our heart, "working for the Lord, not for men, since you know that you will receive an inheritance from the Lord as a reward. It is the Lord Christ you are serving" (Colossians 3:23-24).

What I find interesting about eternal rewards is that when we get to heaven, *we won't want them.* The Bible talks about crowns God promises as rewards to His faithful servants. But the Book of Revelation paints a beautiful picture. When we see Christ, we'll toss all those sparkling tiaras at the feet of Jesus, knowing that *without Him we could do nothing!*

Besides eternal rewards, servanthood gives birth to its own rewards even here and now. We may not always get applause or a plaque to hang on the wall or even a thank you. But God has created us to feel pleasure in service—if our attitude is right. And sometimes we find our own loads lifted by lifting those of others.

Mija, a Korean-born orphan, was adopted by American missionaries who truly modeled servanthood. When she became an adult, she and her husband followed in her parents' footsteps by opening their home "to provide a safe haven for our American GIs and their families." They welcomed people to come anytime for meals, studies, games, or just to talk. "It was great," Mija says. "I felt useful. The Lord taught me to serve others through my home. I tend to keep to myself and crawl in a shell, so the Lord worked wonders in me to crack this old shell of mine to serve others and their needs."

Because of a difficult, hurtful beginning in life, Mija struggled with opening herself to others, fearing she would be hurt again. "But when I was daily concerned with others' hurts and needs," she says, "my needs seemed smaller and less significant. It stretched my faith."

When we feel neglected—as though no one cares—that may be the very time we need to reach out to someone else. We're more sensitive to hurts then, and as we share another person's load, we find our own problems weighing lighter on our shoulders.

Pam from Iowa says, "I just want to be a servant—not only when it's convenient … but regardless of my schedule or agenda."

Servanthood isn't always easy. In fact, Dave Glock, a professor at Emmaus Bible College in Iowa, says, "If you want to know if you have a servant's heart, see how you react when someone treats you like a servant."

The idea of adding a maid's or servant's hat to all our others may be enough to send us babbling to the loony bin. But here's the beauty of it: We can look at all our other hats as part of an integrated whole of servanthood—serving our Lord and King, Jesus Christ, who loved us and gave His life to make ours whole.

That outlook is part of a whole new adventure in God's great wild kingdom....

Study Questions

1. Read Matthew 20:26-28, Philippians 2:4-7, and John 13:1-5. Our culture encourages us to fight for our rights and "look out for #1." But what example does Jesus set for us in this verse? Why do His attitude and actions seem so contrary to what we expect?

2. Read Galatians 5:13-14. How do you think the "serve one another in love" principle sums up the Ten Commandments? (Since it's not practical to try to look at the whole of "the Law and the Prophets" here, it might be good to review at least the Ten Commandments. See Exodus 20:1-17.)

3. Read 1 Samuel 12:24 (if possible read it in the New American Standard Bible). Also read Colossians 3:17 and Matthew 25:40. How do these verses offer motivation and strength for serving Christ and others?

4. Read Mark 9:35 and Philippians 2:3-4. What character quality is the hallmark of a servant? How do we know if we have a servant's heart or not?

5. Read Galatians 6:2 and 10. What are some practical ways we can carry each other's burdens? Our first thoughts of service are to help those in our church family who are in need, and that's biblical. But how do you think our community would be affected if we showed similar thoughtfulness to those around us who don't go to our church and perhaps don't know Christ? What might you do for someone in your neighborhood this week?

6. How do you think we can develop a better sensitivity to each other's needs?

7. How do you think the "serve-one-another-in-love principle" can help us better handle all our many responsibilities as women?

EIGHT

Who Gives Out the Pith Helmets?

My Role as an Adventurer in God's Kingdom

*I love being who God made me! It's a privilege.
To think He even desires to use this one small,
insignificant person astounds me!*
—Mary King
Her hats include those of adult Bible teacher,
AWANA leader, assistant to her husband—
a children's evangelist, mother of three grown
children, grandmother of two.

Martha, who was a single mom for several years, gets lost easily. The politically correct might call her directionally challenged—like me. But whenever Martha's young children would ask her why it was taking so long to get to their destination, she would reply, "Oh, we're just having an adventure." They soon caught on, and whenever they suspected she didn't have a clue where she was going, the kids would ask, "Are we on an adventure, Mom?"

As friends and servants of Christ, we can become confident adventurers, following His path in His kingdom. We, who once were lost, can find a sure purpose for our lives that pulls together all our roles into one meaningful whole. But finding that unfrenzied wholeness of purpose truly can be an adventure!

One of my favorite restaurants is The Rainforest Cafe. In addition to unique food and beverages, the atmosphere is a hoot! Designed to look like a tropical rainforest, the restaurant features huge gnarly trees, a customer-misting waterfall with accompanying rainbow, a starlit sky, and live macaws and cockatoos. Exotic tropical fish frolic in the aquarium arch entryway, and stuffed gorillas beat their chests while emitting macho grunts. Every few minutes the lights flicker, and cracks of thunder challenge conversation.

What tickles me most is that when you ask to be seated, a host assigns your group a name, such as the Rhinoceros party or the Ocelot party. When your table is ready, the host calls out something like this: "Ocelot party of five, your adventure is about to begin!"

In a way, that's how I would characterize my journey with Christ. It's as though the day I put my faith in Him, all the heavenly hosts called out, "Joyce, party of one (someday party of five), your adventure is about to begin."

And what an adventure it has been!

God's "Wild" Kingdom

Have you ever seen safari adventurers with their khaki shirts and shorts and that essential matching headgear—the sturdy pith helmet? I always tease my dad about the one he brought home after World War II from all the heavy fighting he did—in Southern Missouri!

But I can see two advantages in that kind of hat. First, it creates your own personal shade. And second, it protects you from the elements, underbrush, and maybe even the swipe of a ferocious predator's paw.

When we put our lives under God's authority, committed to following His ways and living for Him, we not only begin an adventure, we enter a red-hot battle zone—battles on the home front, battles in the office, battles in schools, and battles in the community. But God offers us some heavy-duty armor, including the (pith) helmet of salvation (see Ephesians 6). With this hat snugly fitted, we can take the heat of all our responsibilities more confidently.

"The Lord watches over you," God promises. "The Lord is your *shade* at your right hand; the sun will not harm you.... *he will watch over your life*; the Lord will watch over your coming and going both now and forevermore" (Psalm 121:5-8, emphasis mine).

In all our rushing around—coming and going—the Lord has promised to stay right with us, sheltering us from anything we can't handle and equipping us to deal with the things we only *think* we can't handle (see 1 Corinthians 10:13). Even Christians who have been brutally persecuted know that nothing can harm our true inner self with God watching over us.

And then, as a sturdy pith helmet protects adventurers from dangers around them, God's helmet of salvation protects the mind within. The Bible tells us that as we trek through our earthly adventure with Him, we need to watch out for attacks from a ferocious natural enemy named Satan, who paces back and forth looking for someone he can have for dinner (see 1 Peter 5:8).

My grandfather died when I was twelve, but I remember one of his favorite sayings: "I steadily refuse to gratify the devil by being discouraged." What a great perspective! Two of the most vulnerable areas to the Enemy's attacks are our minds and our emotional makeup. That's why certainty of our relationship with God and a good knowledge of His Word are so important.

The Confident Adventurer

"The Lord will rescue me from every evil attack and will bring me safely to his heavenly kingdom," writes Timothy. "To him be glory for ever and ever" (2 Timothy 4:18). But when our minds become confused by difficulties we don't understand or emotions fly out of control (whether from overwhelming circumstances or a PMS attack), we need to remind ourselves of the tremendous inheritance we can enjoy already because we are trusting in Christ. The first chapter of Ephesians lists a number of them:

- We are His adopted children with all the rights and privileges thereof (v. 5). He chose us before creation (vv. 4, 11).

- We are blessed with every spiritual blessing (v. 3).

- We are forgiven of all our sins—past, present, and future (v. 7).

- We have been redeemed from sin—bought back. We can live victoriously. It cost Jesus His life (v. 7)!

- We are holy and blameless in His sight—because Christ took the punishment for our sin (v. 4).

- We are recipients of His grace—His generosity. He finds pleasure in giving us all we need (vv. 6-8).

- We have been let in on the mystery of His ultimate goal—to one day bring everything in heaven and earth under the authority of Christ (vv. 9-10).

- We have purpose: to "be" and live in such a way that we bring Him praise and glory (v. 12).

- We have His stamp of ownership on us—the Holy Spirit, who lives within us to comfort and guide us (vv. 13-14).

How can we remain discouraged when we think of all He has done for us and how much it cost Him! We have everything we need to fight the Enemy because greater is He that is in us than he that is in the world (see 1 John 4:4).

But our position in the kingdom is not just a defensive one, fending off Satan's attacks and trying to survive the hurtful things in life. Because we are God's children, servants, and friends, He also gives us assignments to move His kingdom toward the ultimate goal.

Kingdom Assignments

A few years ago some friends told me about a Bible conference they attended. "It was great—so many people soaking up the Word of God together." That is exciting! And I've enjoyed many gatherings like that. But sometimes I think those of us who have been Christians for some time have soaked up a great deal of Scripture, and we need the Word wrung out of us! We've learned much. It's time to pass it on.

When a loved one dies, we naturally want to pay particular attention to that person's last words. We cherish those words and replay them over and over in our minds—especially if the last words were a request. We'll do anything to carry out a loved one's last wishes.

Among Jesus' last words to His disciples before He returned to heaven were these: "Go and make disciples of all nations ... teaching them to obey everything I have commanded you. And surely I am with you always, to the very end of the age" (Matthew 28:18-20).

As far as I know, He has not rescinded that Great Commission. Yet so often we go through our daily schedules without giving thought to how we might do what He asked. It's easy to view those words as only for those who have chosen to become career missionaries. But the Bible implies that being a missionary isn't a choice. It's even more than a command. It's a fact for every Christian. Those of us who have a faith relationship with Jesus Christ *"are* ... Christ's ambassadors" (2 Corinthians 5:20, emphasis mine). The question is, How well are we doing our job?

This became even more real to me when my family moved to a new house some years ago and found that China was right across the street. An extended Chinese family lived there, and two of their children came to know Christ through a Bible club in our yard. Admittedly, we've also missed a lot of opportunities, also, but I believe the Lord wants all of us to change our narrow way of looking at things and see things His way.

Kingdom Vision

When our son was two, I spent a lot of time knitting for our second child, then *in utero*. One day, while I was knitting, Greg came to me all upset because he couldn't find his baseball cap.

I told him it was on top of the bookcase, but he didn't recognize the word.

I tried to motion and explain, but he didn't understand. In those days—due to my "infant-icipation"—it was a lot tougher to get out of a chair than into one. I didn't feel like getting the cap myself, so I called him over to me. Putting his head right up next to mine, I pointed. "See it?" I said.

He smiled and nodded. Then he ran over to the cap and plopped it on top of his head, satisfied at last.

What about you and me? Can we snuggle up close to the Lord and line up our sight with His divine sight so that when He points we see those around us who are hurting and lonely and dying without Him? I believe that if just once we could see this world through His eyes—with His compassion—we would have no trouble serving Him faithfully!

God can use us to pass along His good news to our children, friends, or total strangers—even all of the above—if we'll see this world through His eyes and become sensitive to His prompting.

Mary King says that when she was telling a neighbor about Christ one day, the neighbor became irate, saying Mary sounded like her sister. Knowing that the neighbor faced a torturous eternity if she didn't come to know Christ, Mary tried to talk to her and even gave her a book to read. But the neighbor kept responding the same way.

A few months later, the neighbor died suddenly. "I was shocked," Mary says. "It was a lesson to watch for opportunities and always be ready to speak up for our Lord. I only wish I had been more bold and direct."

This is where it gets sticky. The old saying "You can lead a horse to water, but you can't make it drink" fits here. We can't make people trust Christ. And we may wonder if we've done *all* we could to lead them to where they could put their faith in

Him. But we can be on the lookout for opportunities, ask our Father for boldness, and leave the results to Him.

Kingdom Perspective

I can imagine someone saying, "Thanks a lot. Now I've got the guilt of not telling others about Christ in addition to my guilt of not managing all my other hats well." But actually, seeing the importance of our role in His Great Commissioning (Matthew 28:18-20) can help us focus on which hats we should be wearing and which ones we can let go. It can also help us gain an eternal perspective on everything we do.

One mother of five—who has survived breast cancer and widowhood in her thirties—says, "I feel I have done a good job as a mother, raising my kids in the Lord, and I have witnessed to others. Still—maybe it's low self-esteem speaking, but—I don't feel used of God. I feel I am surviving day to day, moment to moment."

When you come down to it, though, we all have to live moment to moment, don't we? "Blessed are those whose strength is in [God], who have set their hearts on pilgrimage [adventure?]. As they pass through the Valley … they make it a place of springs.... They go from strength to strength, till each appears before God" (Psalm 84:5-7, bracketed additions mine).

God says that in the adventure of life, when we go to Him for help, we can live from strength to strength instead of from crisis to crisis—as I naturally tend to do. And His supernatural strength becomes evident to those around us. This young mother later mentioned that with all she's been through, "people feel free to come to me with their problems." Isn't that being used of God? She has a depth of insight that others don't have because of the valley in which she has lived.

And what about her children? How God must be using her in their lives, demonstrating that He is real and that He cares for them even in the toughest imaginable circumstances! In his third letter in Scripture, the apostle John said, "I have no greater joy than to hear that my children are walking in the truth" (v. 4). I can't imagine any greater joy for a mom or anyone who teaches others spiritual truth.

Jeannie Cedar, a California woman, says that the Lord is teaching her to do quickly whatever He brings to mind. "If I obey quickly, I can't analyze it away. And if I make a fool of myself for Him, that should never be a problem."

Once, after moving into a new neighborhood, Jeannie felt she should invite her neighbor over for coffee. She called and the neighbor came. About two weeks later Jeannie felt an urgency to invite the neighbor a second time.

When the neighbor sat down at the dining room table, she noticed a Bible verse Jeannie had written out. "You know," the neighbor said, "I find I can't understand the Bible. Do you?"

Jeannie ran and got her *Life Application Bible* and said, "Let me read a verse to you from here." She read, "Don't worry about anything, instead pray" (Philippians 4:6). Then she read the application that followed in that study Bible.

"She was so pleased," Jeannie says. "It was the Lord working in her heart." Jeannie and her husband had been praying daily for this woman and other neighbors, and now they were seeing God answer.

After Jeannie mentioned that she could get a Bible like that for her neighbor (at a special price) if she would read it, the neighbor eagerly accepted the offer. "She's still reading it," Jeannie says, "and God's at work!"

All of this began years earlier, when her children were small, because Jeannie had responded to God's prompting to "get out of my four walls each day," as she put it, "—a call to a neighbor, a letter, anything." And about once a week she attempted to invite one person over as her own outreach in the neighborhood.

Kingdom Challenges

Unfortunately, many times we get so preoccupied with personal problems, family struggles, and job frustrations that we have trouble focusing on the main reason God has left us here—to help others find Christ.

A respected church leader in China told a former pastor of mine that the believers in China persistently pray for American Christians. They feel that the physical persecution Chinese Christians have suffered is not much different from the family pain suffered by many Americans. While the Chinese church is thriving through its persecution, however, we're not making much headway in introducing others to Christ.

When our problems rise above our purpose, we become unbalanced and sidelined from the kingdom battle. But if we keep an eye on the goal—to know Christ and to tell others about Him—we can trust Him to help us through the difficult times.

In college when my photography instructor analyzed students' photos in front of the class, he never said something was bad and never referred to a problem area. He would say something like, "The challenge in this photo is …" I like that. Problems can defeat us. But with my competitive spirit, I'm always ready for a challenge—especially if I can turn it over to my Creator who made me and knows the outcome before I even know there's a "challenge."

The three great questions of all people throughout history have been: Who am I? Why am I here? and Where am I going?

As Christian women, we find our identity, purpose, and future in our Lord Jesus Christ. This Commission He gave us brings a wholeness of purpose to all our many hats. Our purpose is to help others answer those three questions through a personal relationship with Jesus Christ. The Great Commission can also help us weed out those things that don't accomplish His purposes for us. But we need to be open, perhaps, to some new definitions of what it means to be used of God.

Kingdom Nudging

Rosalie, a nurse for many years, decided to take a less stressful job to create more balance in her life. Now she works in a mall, where she waits on many of the same people every day. Thanks to her winsome personality and genuine concern for people, some of her "regulars" talk to her about family and marriage problems. And Rosalie takes advantage of those openings. "Sometimes just a quick comment can get them thinking on the right track," she says.

We may not present the entire message of Christ each time we talk to people, but if we nudge them one step closer to a relationship with Christ, we're effective adventurers in the kingdom.

Linda Hansen, who works in a college library, says she believes that every person with whom she comes into contact is someone she can influence for the Lord. Though she struggles with her human nature and imperfections, she says, "It is my prayer that they will want to know the Lord because of His Spirit working in me to be all I should be."

This year Linda has made a point of spending more time with her work-study students each day. She talks to them about schedules, goals, friendships, and struggles. "I've started to tell them I will be praying for them for specific situations, and they thank me and continue to share with me."

Pam from Iowa says, "I feel God uses me most when I put aside my busy life and slow down long enough to listen to a friend, encourage her, follow up with her, and continue to support her."

We don't have to do "great things" for God. But God can use anything we do for Him in great ways!

Kingdom Investment

Last summer my sister Jeanne told me that the Lord had brought a question to her mind that she wanted to pass along: What has God invested in you?

As I pondered the question, a second thought came to mind: "What kind of return is He getting on His investment?"

King David wrote, "Lord, you have assigned me my portion and my cup; you have made my lot secure. The boundary lines have fallen for me in pleasant places; surely I have a delightful inheritance" (Psalm 16:5-6).

Yes, I've experienced crises and heartbreaks, but God has

been so good through it all. And my relationship with Him is even stronger.

In addition to all those treasures from Ephesians mentioned earlier, God's Holy Spirit has given each of us at least one spiritual gift—a special ability we received directly from Him when we began our relationship with Christ. We can use these presents from God to serve Him and build up others in His kingdom.

These gifts, at least in part, are listed in Romans 12, 1 Corinthians 12, Ephesians 4, and 1 Peter 4. They may or may not coincide with natural strengths and talents. But God gives us gifts that He knows we can use—gifts He wants us to use—for Him. With these gifts He equips us for service in the kingdom.

There is nothing more frustrating than giving someone a present and then watching her put it away for safekeeping, never to use or wear it. Yet sometimes we must frustrate God in regard to the gifts He gives us. We don't look for them or we ignore them or we simply put them on the shelf to be used someday—when we're not so busy with "the tyranny of the present."

On the other hand, when we struggle with our too-many hats, it may be because we're spreading ourselves too thin, not zeroing in on our areas of giftedness.

My dad tells a joke about a woman who was baking her husband some frozen pizza for a snack one night. "Honey," she called to him in the other room, "how many pieces do you want me to cut the pizza into—six or eight?" To which he replied, "You'd better cut it into six. I don't think I could eat eight."

OK, the joke's a groaner, yet I'm afraid many of us women

have picked up that strange logic. There are no extra brownie points in heaven for cutting ourselves up into more pieces. In fact, the more areas in which we try to be effective, the less effective we actually become in each one.

But as each of us gets to know how she has been created and what God has invested in her—spiritual gifts, talents, heritage, family, and even the painful things we've come through—we can begin to see a "wholeness" to our service in the kingdom. And that can tell us what kind of return God is getting on His investment.

In her book *Giftedness: Discovering Your Areas of Strength*, Marcia L. Mitchell says, "The gifts are woven into our lives, but we have to allow God to use those gifts whenever they are needed.... The body of Christ is like a tapestry in progress. The threads are all there, and when God wants to utilize a certain color, though it may be at a most unexpected time, He reaches through and pulls the thread of that color to the front. We, the thread, need to be pliable and willing."[1]

Kingdom Under Attack

Ironically, I've noticed that our areas of giftedness often become our Enemy's favorite battlefield. For instance, I believe that one of my spiritual gifts is faith. I have a keen vision and tenacious confidence in God's ability to do impossible things, yet one of my greatest areas of weakness is worry. My former boss has the gift of discernment and the ability to speak truth in a confusing situation, yet she admits that her greatest struggle is fear of what others will think of her if she speaks the truth. Another woman has the gift of hospitality yet battles busyness, procrastination, and pride issues that often keep her from open-ing her home to others.

Satan would like to discourage us from using our spiritual gifts, for they are the supernatural means of serving God in all His power. They build others up while Satan wants to tear us down. But we can steadily refuse to gratify the devil (either by being discouraged or by being sidetracked from using those gifts) because we know that our God in us is more powerful than our Enemy in the world.

The battle lines in the Kingdom have been drawn: The King of Kings (our Lord Jesus Christ) versus the Prince of Darkness (Satan). But we know the final outcome. According to Revelation 12, Satan knows his time is brief. God will win. But until then, our Creator has outfitted each of us with our unique equipment to bring about that final victory—whether we're directly involved in bringing others to a personal relationship with Him or building up the troops or tending the wounded or all three.

Our Corner of the Kingdom

Each of us has a mission field. A sphere of influence. A sea in which we are to be fisherwomen for Christ. Our sphere of ser-vice can be far or near—or far come near.

My friend Linda Schmidt and her husband, parents of two teenagers of their own, welcome college students from other countries to live with them during the school year. To anyone from another culture, a loving Christian family is probably the best advertisement for a personal relationship with Jesus Christ. In addition, Linda has become a highly skilled garage-sale shopper, ferreting out like-new discarded clothing, furniture, dishes, and other necessities for relocated refugees in her community.

Whatever our corner of the kingdom, we have the privilege of not only living the truth of Christ's life-changing power but telling it as well.

The Christian fish symbol on my bank checks has prompted several conversations in check-out lanes—especially when the cashier wasn't particularly busy.

A friend of mine can easily turn polite conversation on a plane or in a taxi into an opportunity to talk about Christ's love. She zeroes in on the current struggles of her captive audiences and lets them know that God cares about them and wants to be part of their lives.

The early death of my sister's husband actually gave her boldness to ask his coworkers and business associates where their soul would be for eternity if it were their bodies in that casket.

Even if we're nervous talking about spiritual things, we can ease into reaching out through any of the many tools now available. Here are some tools God is using to bring others to Him:

The *Houses of Prayer* organization encourages pockets of Christians in each neighborhood to gather regularly to pray for those who live around them. Participants let neighbors know they're praying for them and ask if there are any concerns they can pray about. Hundreds of people all over the world have come to know Christ through this outreach. For more information contact Mission 21 H.O.P.E. (Houses of Prayer Everywhere) at Box 141312, Grand Rapids, MI 49514, or (616) 453-9311.

Moms in Touch is another group with a similar approach. Mothers (and grandmothers) of school-age children meet regularly to pray for their kids, schools, teachers, principals, and school districts. In addition to prayer, they also bring or send notes of encouragement and gifts, such as baked goods or fruit, to teachers and principals. For more information contact Moms in Touch International, Box 1120, Poway, CA 92074, or (619) 486-4065.

The Jesus Video Project offers a biblically sound film of the life of Christ that many people have used successfully even in their own homes. The film clearly presents who Christ is and how He can change a person's life. For more information contact the Jesus Video Project, 24600 Arrowhead Springs Rd., San Bernardino, CA 92414.

Pursuit magazine, mentioned briefly in the previous chapter, is an attractive full-color magazine centered around the personal needs many unbelievers struggle with, such as fear, hopelessness, pain, uncertainty, failure, meaninglessness, and relationships. Even those who don't feel they can talk to others about Christ can leave a magazine like this behind on public transportation or in a waiting room—with a little prayer that God will use it. Or they can hand a copy to a friend who's going through a tough time and suggest she read an article that relates and discuss it later. For a free sample copy or information about gift subscriptions or discounted bulk rates, contact *Pursuit* at 901 E. 78th Street, Minneapolis, MN 55420-1360, or call (612) 853-1750.

Sports Spectrum is a similar magazine with articles and profiles of sports figures designed to encourage sports fans to consider Christ's place in their lives. For more information contact *Sports Spectrum* subscriptions, Box 37120, Boone,

IA, 50037, or e-mail to magsub@sport.org.

The many tools available can help us get the message out. We just need to become faithful servants and use them. Outreach isn't "another hat," but a way of responding to the relationships and opportunities that are already there—being the salt and light in the mission field around us. Some scholars have translated the *go ye* with the words *as you are going*.... In his book *Roaring Lambs,* Bob Briner asks a pointed question: "Can we be all Christ expects us to be in a closet?"

Perhaps your mission field is the woman who works at the desk in the next cubicle. Maybe it's the neighbor down the street who just lost her husband to cancer. Perhaps yours are the little "fish" who swim in your bathtub on Saturday night.

"Whatever you do, whether in word or deed," Paul writes, "do it all in the name of the Lord Jesus, giving thanks to God the Father through him" (Colossians 3:17).

It's a Jungle Out There!

In what "wild kingdom" has God put you? It's a jungle out there—it's true. But we can be sure of who we are in Christ and know for certain that He is with us no matter where we go and what problems we face. "I have set the Lord always before me," David says. "Because he is at my right hand, I will not be shaken" (Psalm 16:8). Armed with that knowledge, we can commit ourselves to enjoying life's adventure, confident that there's no challenge we can't handle with Christ by our side.

Of course, the older we get, the more *irksome* some of those challenges become....

Study Questions

1. Read Matthew 28:18-20 and 2 Corinthians 5:20. Why doesn't the Lord whisk us off to heaven after we come to know Him? For what purpose has He left us here? How do you think that mindset can help us choose which hats (responsibilities) we take on?

2. Read 1 Peter 5:8, 2 Timothy 4:18, and 1 John 4:4. We might view ourselves as adventurers in God's wild kingdom—adventurers with a job to do. But we also have an Enemy who delights in sidetracking us. What do we learn in these verses about our Enemy and our relationship to him?

3. Read Psalm 121:5-8, 1 Corinthians 10:13, and Ephesians 6:10-18. What protection does God give us in fighting our Enemy?

4. Read Ephesians 1:4-14. What are some resources we have right now for doing the things God asks of us? How does it make you feel to know you have all this at your disposal?

5. Read 2 Timothy 1:5 and 3 John verse 4. The Letter of 2 Timothy was written by Paul to a young man named Timothy who grew up in a family with at least three

generations of strong faith. In light of these two verses and Matthew 28:18-20, what is another way we can view motherhood?

6. Read 2 Timothy 1:6-7. What is our responsibility for the gifts God gives us to build up His kingdom?

7. Read Psalm 84:5-7. How does this verse compare with the way many of us tend to live our lives?

NINE

Does a Black Veil Go With Everything?

~

My Role in Aging Gracefully

As we get older, laughter and a good sense of humor play a bigger part. When my husband and I go someplace in our car, I'll say, "You remember our names, and I'll remember where we are going."

—Vel McNeal
Her hats include those of real estate agent,
wife of a real estate agent, mother of
four grown children, grandmother of nine,
hostess to many visitors in her home.

"**G**racefully? Did you say gracefully?" one of my cousins responded. "No way! I'm fighting it every inch (ooh! and I do mean inch) of the way. They say wisdom comes with age, but so do a lot of other things. I vainly cover the gray, but the mustache is the toughest thing to handle!"

Many of us can identify—and she's only in her early forties!

Several years ago, I heard author Madeleine L'Engle speak here in Minneapolis. As she took her place behind the lectern, she took off one pair of glasses and put on another, saying, "They tell me after forty it's maintenance, maintenance, maintenance."

Perhaps we hate aging so much because our body's deterioration forces us to deal with our own mortality. As someone has said, "From the moment we are born we begin to die."

But no matter when or how we struggle with aging, we need a good sense of humor, confidence, and good support—and I don't mean Wonderbras and control-top pantyhose!

When I was complaining about getting old one day, my husband said, "You're not getting old. You're just a spring chicken. *Late* spring—but..." That wasn't exactly the type of support I was looking for. I guess it might qualify as humor, but it certainly didn't boost my confidence. In revenge I keep reminding him he graduated from high school before I celebrated my eleventh birthday!

My full-figure frame swells with pride, however, when people gape in utter amazement that our three kids are all in their twenties. "Why, you don't look old enough to have kids that age!" they exclaim. Or, "What'd you do, start having babies when you were twelve?"

"Old" is relative, I guess. For instance, I never liked antiques—especially early in our marriage. I couldn't understand why people spent hours wading through junkyards and moving sales and antique shops and flea markets to unearth something old—something another rational human being threw away because it had outlived its usefulness.

I grew up with old stuff—hand-me-downs and secondhand-store clothing and furniture. When I got married, I wanted a fresh start with everything brand new. Of course, I quickly discovered how costly everything new was.

But my mind remained in "new-tral" for several years before I suspected a defection. I started appreciating the beautiful woodwork and craftsmanship in a few family heirlooms. Soon I was admiring Victorian houses and "gingerbread" detailing along the eaves. I started browsing antique shops as though they were museums.

I'm still not a collector, and I don't spend much time antique-store hopping, but I began wondering at this retro phase. When I mentioned it to my husband, he responded with the droll comment, "Oh, you're just glad to find anything older than you are."

Over Which Hill?

I'm now peeking around the corner at fifty, so it's natural to be thinking about getting older. But when I learned that my nephew's wife—still in her twenties—is bothered by aging, that made me feel even older!

When did you start feeling old?

- I felt extremely old when we visited friends far away and their youngest son asked what they should call us: "Mr. and Mrs. Ellis? Uncle Steve and Aunt Joyce? The old folks?"

- My daughter started feeling old when kids she once baby-sat graduated from high school.

- A friend says age didn't bother her until she hit sixty. But her "Big 6-O" put her on a grueling track to retirement. "Since then I've learned to never say I am tired, never groan over a project, never be sick—because surely it would be chalked up to aging."

So the one-two punch of aging—physical and emotional—can hit us at almost any time past high school. And we become creative in our ways of dealing with it.

Helen, a Texan, says she marked the occasion of her fiftieth birthday by inviting everyone to bring a crying towel so they could mourn with her.

A friend from our church in her thirties admits to an unusual experiment. "I tried putting tape over my ever-growing laugh lines to try to train my face to laugh in a less damaging way," she says. "I looked so funny that I laughed probably two more years onto my face!"

For some reason, in our culture, aging *is* funny. One of the most common ways to celebrate age landmarks is by embarrassing the person with an "over-the-hill party"—whichever hill may be the most devastating to each person.

A number of years ago when a friend turned thirty, her husband arranged a party, complete with gag gifts like Metamucil, a walking cane, and an old-lady hat with its used-to-be-perky little veil. He ordered a cake with black frosting and *Over the Hill* piped in white. When he went to pick up the cake, however, there was a large crack right down the middle! The baker apologized, but the husband burst out laughing. "No, it's perfect!" he cried.

Mind Over Matter

Dozens of platitudes float around us, trying to help us feel better about this aging process. One of my mom's favorites is "Aging is just mind over matter. If you don't mind, it doesn't matter."

But the physical maladies that accompany aging can't be totally erased with a Pollyanna outlook. One of my aunts touted the benefits of humor but added an ironic note: "I don't think aging would be a problem for me if I were in better health."

I'm beginning to understand. Since I've started keeping company with the two Itis brothers, Arthr and Tendon, I now find myself needing help getting into the car and avoiding stairs as though they were poison. And my futile attempts to control my body temperature give me a whole new appreciation for the fashion concept of "layering." I've since bought a new counted cross-stitch pattern that reads: Real women don't have hot flashes; they have power surges!

We can't wish the aches and pains and wrinkles and bulges away. We can't even control them sometimes. (I will admit, however, that I'm usually first in line to audition the treatments our Creator has allowed researchers to discover so I can keep up this rat race I hate!) But we need to look to the One who made us this way for perspective among the symptoms that make us feel old:

"[God] knows how we are formed, he remembers that we are dust." The Bible is so flattering, isn't it? "But from everlasting to everlasting the Lord's love is with those who fear him, and his righteousness with their children's children—with those who keep his covenant and remember to obey his precepts" (Psalm 103:14-18). I like the old King James Version here, too: "He knoweth our frame." Isn't that comforting?

When I was discussing aging with my ophthalmologist friend, he said med school taught him the effects of aging on the human body. "I just didn't expect it to happen so soon on mine."

God knows better than our doctors how aging is affecting us. So we can trust Him to give us the strength and support we need for the tasks ahead—or we can accept the limitations we can't change and learn to say *no* when we have to. He doesn't expect more out of us than our body, mind, and spirit can do. Why should we feel guilty about saying *no* when other people ask too much?

The mother of two and wife of a children's evangelist, Mary King, says, "I've had to say *no* to other well-meaning Christians who want to commit me to other areas of service. I'm fully committed already plus I have to fit my personal life in, so I have to hold the line."

When my sister was pregnant with her "bonus baby" nearly ten years after her previous "caboose," she often commented about how much more difficult it was to be pregnant at almost-forty than at almost-thirty. She had to learn to adjust her expectations as well as her activities to accommodate "her frame."

It's a matter of adjusting, not giving up. Our minds can trick us into thinking that we're less useful to God or that our life is nearly over simply because we have new adjustments to make.

Terry, a thirty-something Iowa mom, tells about the time she participated in a two-hundred-yard race. *No problem*, thought this woman who used to run track. But she choked on her competitors' dust. "My body said *no*," she recalls. "I forgot I was twenty-five years older."

Pam, also from Iowa, says it has helped her to "focus on spiritual aging—which only improves—rather than on physical aging—which gets ugly!"

"Therefore we do not lose heart," wrote the apostle Paul. "Though outwardly we are wasting away, yet inwardly we are being renewed day by day" (2 Corinthians 4:16). As we expose ourselves to the Scriptures and allow ourselves to become more and more like our Lord Jesus Christ, He renews our spirit, and the beauty works its way outward. So I've made it my goal to spend at least as much time on spiritual maintenance as I do on physical maintenance each day.

One of the most beautiful women I know is Margaret Hanson, an eighty-plus-year-old widow—though you'd never guess her age. She meets with several young women each week for one-on-one Bible studies, works with children's programs, and helps in other areas at church. A few years ago her grandson remarked, "Grandma, why do your hands look so much older than your face?" Margaret replied, "Maybe because my hands are always so busy."

I think the time she spends reading and studying God's Word is a renewing, rejuvenating agent that shines out in that young face, too.

Is There Life After Feeling Old?

Squeezed grapes, with age, can become fine wine or bitter, moldy juice. I'd rather be fine wine. And I delight in some of the role models the Lord has put in my life. Some of my dearest friends are a generation older.

Ruth McKinney, a retired secretary in Illinois who got her college degree just a few years ago, gives this advice: "You are what you will become. If you're cranky and complaining now, you will get worse!"

I know what she means. Some people have *enjoyed* ill health for years! Others sing a pity ditty for each new ailment. A sixtyish friend of mine says she's tired of hearing her friends' "organ" recitals—where, what year, and why each one was removed.

Ironically, it was my hairstylist, DeDe, who passed along

some verses I had never looked at from the perspective of aging: "Your beauty should not come from outward adornment, such as braided hair and the wearing of gold jewelry and fine clothes. Instead, it should be that of your inner self, the unfading beauty of a gentle and quiet spirit, which is of great worth in God's sight" (1 Peter 3:3-4).

What great insight—especially for a woman who knows the hairs of my head and how many more are turning gray each month! I don't try to color them. I'm too cheap and too lazy to keep it up. Besides, some women pay a lot of money to get their hair "frosted," and God does mine for free!

I must admit gray hairs can trigger vanity. I'll never forget the time a young woman picked me up at the airport in Chicago, where I was to speak for a conference. Caught up in conversation, I didn't realize that my amiable chauffeur seemed to have lost her way exiting the freeway. We drove around in circles for several minutes before she pulled into a parking lot to get her bearings. When I leaned over to look at the directions the conference director dictated by phone, I saw these words at the top of the paper: "Hair grayer than in picture."

Eventually we reached our destination, but I still tease the conference director about the description. She insists she said "shorter," not "grayer"—but do they sound anything alike to you?

Gray hairs can get to us, but I now use them as object lessons to my grown children. Holding out a silver strand, I name some errant behavior that caused that one to turn pale in fright—little things like when they put their toddler sister in the dryer and turned it on. "It was only for a few seconds," they defend. But it left its mark on me—and Little Sis—forever!

That's why I find great comfort in this promise: "Even to

your old age and gray hairs I am he … who will sustain you. I have made you and I will carry you; I will sustain you and I will rescue you" (Isaiah 46:4).

Even through the scrambled brains of menopause? I ask.

Then I think back over the years. He has sustained me and comforted and guided me through so much: that first year of marital adjustment, miscarriage, life-threatening medical emergencies with our children, refereeing countless sibling quibblings, kissing away a myriad of child-size tears, belt-tightening exercises, interpersonal struggles, questionable choices of our teenagers, staring into the darkness of 2:30 A.M. wondering where they were, weathering my own self-doubts in my many roles, and times of wandering away from the Lord. If He can handle all that, surely I can trust Him to get me through the gray hairs, hassles, and other horrors of aging.

Ad In

In tennis, the server's point after a tie (deuce) is called *ad in* or *advantage* to the server. That's where we are when we move ahead into the "older" age bracket. Despite all the obvious disadvantages, we're moving ahead to a place of numerous advantages. My friend and writing colleague Sharon Sheppard shared a few perks of getting older:

- I'm smarter now.
- I'm more mature.
- I'm still busy, but I have more discretionary time and fewer labor-intensive responsibilities for the family.
- I can do as I please more often.

- My husband and I can invest more time in our relationship.

So hang in there, young women. There is a glimmer of hope on the other side of the diaper stacker.

I Think I Shall Have a Midlife Crisis

After I lost my dream job more than a year ago, one day I consciously decided, "I think I shall have a midlife crisis. I've worked hard for it. I deserve it!" If the usual life span for human beings is "three-score and ten" or seventy, according to Psalm 90:10, midlife should be about 35, right? I was long overdue. It was time to do something totally irresponsible, something wild and crazy.

But I was so exhausted I couldn't think up anything wild, crazy, or irresponsible to do! The most outlandish thing I did that summer was making myself ride "The Screaming Eagle" roller coaster at Six Flags in St. Louis. (Actually, quite a feat for someone who can hardly climb a step stool without a vertigo attack!)

It's hard to have a midlife crisis when you're confident in who you are—and when you're already a little wild and crazy to begin with. But some women come to midlife or a job loss or retirement, and they thrash around in the waters of life as though they were going down for the third time. They have no confidence because they don't know who they are.

- If your identity is tied to your looks, what happens when the sagging and wrinkling begins? Who are you?

- If your identity is tied to your athleticism, what happens when injuries sideline you or your bones and muscles beg to go into retirement? Who are you?

• If your identity is tied to your job, what happens when you lose that job or you retire? Who are you?

• If your identity is tied to your children, what happens when they demonstrate they can function with a modicum of maturity without you? Who are you?

All this points back to our identity as individual women with unique personalities, interests, gifts, and talents. We can avoid midlife washout—and even some marital difficulties—if we're confident in who we are and nurture our own lives while we're serving those around us.

Maybe we can turn our skirmishes with aging into reminders to plan for the future—not just financially but activity-wise. If we're comfortable with who we are now, we need not fear anything in the future.

Laughing at the Days to Come

Indeed, humor, confidence, and support give us that three-point stability we need to maneuver through maturity—and beyond!

We can seek support from our friends, a spouse if we're married, our extended family, and sometimes even our kids! But above all, our support comes from the Lord. One of my first growing up moments spiritually came during one of our youngest child's real-life E.R. experiences. In the midst of that crisis, the verse that awakened my trust in God's promised support was this: "The eternal God is your refuge, and underneath are the everlasting arms" (Deuteronomy 33:27).

Because our God is all-powerful and eternal, we have a strength unknown to those who don't trust Him. But we need to learn how to tap into that strength. Remember the Bible's role-model woman in Proverbs 31? Clothed with strength and dignity, she can laugh at the days to come (v. 25). Why can she laugh? Because, over her lifetime, the strength and dignity developed through her growing relationship with God eliminates worry about her body's little betrayals.

That word *dignity* worries me a little, though. Does it mean no fun? Wouldn't that contradict the "laugh at the days to come" part? The King James Version uses the word *honor* for *dignity* here, and after consulting a Bible scholar friend regarding the background of the word, I think we could paraphrase the verse this way: She wears her character—her inner strength and inner attractiveness—on her sleeve.

She sounds like a well-adjusted, peaceful woman, doesn't she?

A Few Don'ts

So if we want to be strong, peaceful, attractive women as we move into that "older" category, are there any warnings to heed? Here are a few my friends have passed along:

- Don't think you have to give advice or your opinion on every subject—unless you're asked.
- Don't wallow in your emotions.
- Don't get grumpy and close-minded.
- Don't fear getting old. (I pray the Lord will preserve my mind, and I try to take good care of my body.)

- Don't let slower mean lazier. Do a good job on whatever you do.

My favorite comes from my Aunt Claire: "Don't focus on what you *can't* do. Focus on all the things you *can* do, and be as active as possible. I now have volumes of memories of active and exhausting experiences, which I can enjoy while I'm resting in bed!"

P.S. Grandma's Not Off Her Rocker Yet!

When I started writing this book, I realized there was one hat many women wear that I couldn't discuss from experience—a granny cap. Then shortly before Mother's Day our daughter and son-in-law invited us and his parents for dinner. At each table setting little place cards waited. Mine had a flying stork carrying precious cargo and trailing a banner that read: Grandma Ellis.

"Oh, my goodness," I repeated over and over. I knew what this meant. My husband knew what it meant. Our checkbook balance was in trouble!

But I've been watching grandmothers around me for quite some time now, and grandmotherhood fascinates me:

- Grandmas can be annoying with their 342 pictures of Grandbaby in every pose from "modeling hopeful" to "I can't wait to get out of this stupid outfit so I can get the cookie you promised me."

- Grandmas can be overindulgent. Secret Agent 003, licensed to spoil, they also enjoy free return privileges.

- Grandmas can also pass along spiritual values—sometimes

new direction for grandchildren if their parents don't have a good relationship with the Lord, sometimes reinforcement of things the grandkids have learned at home.

- Grandmas can build up their adult children by applauding the good job they're doing in raising their little ones.

- Grandmas can learn a lot about unconditional love from their grandchildren. "No matter how we blow it," my sister Jan says, "they love us anyway!"

- Grandmas can relearn, through the eyes of their grandchildren, what's important in life—having an ultra tidy house or playing games with people you love.

Again, my Aunt Claire offers me some wonderful aspects of grandmotherhood to look forward to:

"Not being busy about household duties, a grandma has time to read stories, play games, and tell the children about life long ago to give them a connection with past generations. Grandmas get to experience the best behavior and can compliment more often than scold. Being a grandma means taking a slow walk and examining every bug and worm, explaining why God made them. Being a grandma means being surprised at the sweet bouquet of wildflowers held out to her in a small fist. Grandma's words of correction are often as effective as a parent's discipline, for a child usually doesn't want to make Grandma sad."

Psalm 71:18 says, "Even when I am old and gray, do not forsake me, O God"—He's promised He won't, but if we remind Him it may help *us* to remember—"Till I declare your power to the next generation, your might to all who are to come."

I can't wait to tell *our* next generation about our awesome God!

Better Than the Alternative?

People say aging is better than the alternative (death), but I don't think so—at least for the person who is trusting Jesus Christ. Paul said, "For to me, to live is Christ and to die is gain" (Philippians 1:21), so I have nothing to fear. I know so many people in heaven now that I'm looking forward to the time the Lord tells me I've "outlived my usefulness" here.

Several years ago, when asked by Phil Donahue how old she was, Erma Bombeck said she was somewhere between estrogen and death. I guess I'm in that neighborhood, too, but I'm glad that researchers have found some therapies to help smooth the transitions. And I'm also grateful that Someone is waiting for me on the other side, eager to see me and give me a big hug.

The more painful this life gets, the more we find ourselves longing for our true happily-ever-after home where there's no more arthritis or cancer or high blood pressure—not even laugh lines!

So I'm trying to keep His perspective on aging, trusting His promise that if I keep submitting myself to Him and doing what He asks, someday I'll hear those precious words, "Well done, my good and faithful servant."

In the meantime, however....

Study Questions

1. Read 2 Corinthians 4:16-17. Some of us worry about wrinkles and gray hairs more than others do. But in what practical ways do you think we can be rejuvenated from the inside out? What is our ultimate hope if our hearts belong to God? At what age do you think a woman should begin these spiritual beauty treatments?

2. Read 1 Peter 3:3-4. According to these verses, what can we focus on to minimize the effects of aging? What attitudes and actions can make us beautiful inside and out?

3. Read Deuteronomy 33:27 and Psalm 103:14-18. What characteristics of God do you see in these verses? How can this knowledge help us face the aging process with more confidence?

4. Read Isaiah 46:4. This verse can sound humorous, but it's important to note that the promise here comes from our Creator. What three things does He promise as we get older? (Remember, we're getting older every day, whether we like it or not!) How do these specific promises show us that He knows our changing needs as we get older?

5. Read Psalm 71:18. Whether or not God allows us to live until we're old and gray, what is our responsibility to the next generation?

6. Read Proverbs 31:25. What character qualities in a woman help her face the future with confidence? Why do you think these two qualities are so important? How can we develop them or where do they come from?

7. Read Philippians 1:21-24. Perhaps one reason we don't like getting old is that as we get older we have to face our own mortality. Why does a Christian sometimes feel torn between the thought of living and dying? If we have a personal relationship with Jesus Christ, why are we not afraid of death?

TEN

Will You P-l-ease Let Me in Front of the Mirror?

How Do I View My Many Hats?

*I love the chance to wear 500 hats! Also to know
that I hold a lot of our family together.*
—DeDe Schmidt
Her hats include those of hairstylist,
wife of a civil engineer, mother of three
children under the age of nine.

I'll never forget the time I helped a friend buy a dress for an elegant banquet. Neither of us was married, but she had dated Tom, a nice-looking fellow from church, off and on for several months. So she asked him if he would escort her to the business-required event. I knew how much she liked Tom, so when she emerged from the fitting room in this soft, black velvet, form-fitting gown trimmed in exquisite black lace, we agreed she had no choice but to buy it—even though its price tag equaled more than two weeks' worth of my salary. She earned more than I did, but even she swallowed hard at the price. Besides, the snooty salesclerk acted as if we shouldn't even be looking at dresses in that price range, so, of course, we couldn't let her know she was right!

We bantered back and forth about the cost but finally decided my friend would never find another dress that looked so perfect on her, and Tom was worth it!

Tom *would have been* worth it, except he stood her up. Because of his tight schedule, he had arranged to meet her at the banquet hall. But he never came. So there she was, alone in a crowd, wearing that expensive dress, which she couldn't even return. I guess Tom wasn't worth it! But our shopping trip was one we'll never forget!

Millinery Window Shopping

Unfortunately, with our "born-to-shop" mentality, we often go window shopping for more hats to juggle. We see a hat on someone else that we would like to wear, and we put it on. But it isn't us. We try to make it fit and often ignore what it will cost us. That's when we get into trouble.

Many years ago, I attended a luncheon featuring actress Jeanette Clift George. Jeanette, who played Corrie ten Boom in the movie *The Hiding Place*, told about her early days as a Christian. Admiring her friend Marge's talent and service, Jeanette prayed, "Lord, I want to be a 'Marge.'"

"I already have a Marge," the Lord seemed to reply. "And she's doing a very good job at it. I need a Jeanette."

Some of our "too many hats" may be our own fault. When God is the one who puts those hats there—when He gives us various assignments and talents—He expects us to use them. But He always equips us beforehand for anything He asks us to do.

It's true that our hats change over the years, depending on

our stage of life. But I think it's also true that sometimes we store away some of our hats in hatboxes or on the shelf—hats God wants us to enjoy but ones we are afraid or reluctant to use.

Yet over and over in Scripture God tells us not to fear. He is with us. We can trust Him. He's in control. And He loves to see us wearing our hat gifts well.

What Lovely Chapeaux!

As a woman I can be confident because God created me—a unique creation. I don't have to compete with other women (much less men) or be jealous of their talents or circumstances because I am the woman God created me to be. I choose to enjoy my intuitive, relational, and nurturing qualities, allowing God to love others through me.

As a wife I choose to honor my commitment to my husband and love him with actions even when I don't feel very loving toward him. Depending on God for wisdom and strength, I choose to be a helper suitable for him rather than trying to change him into my image of what a perfect husband should be. And I choose to pray for him and his concerns as much as my own.

As a mom I stand in awe that God has entrusted these particular children to me at this particular time. I'm grateful that God is everywhere, watching over them when I can't. I trust Him for wisdom and strength for each day, each challenge, each "phase" my kids are going through. I choose to replace worry with trust and fear with confidence because I know He is in control.

As a working woman (at home or abroad) I thank God for the good feeling of accomplishment that work brings—whether it's a business meeting run smoothly or a hurting coworker comforted lovingly or a kitchen floor scrubbed meticulously (that I know will soon again wear spilled juice and heel marks). Relying on God to help me keep my priorities straight, I choose to plunge into each day's work with faith, integrity, and fun. And, saying *no* to guilt, I commit myself to getting the rest and personal times out I need to supply the necessary energy for my stress-a-day tasks.

As a daughter and daughter-in-law I choose to love my parents and in-laws unconditionally, to live in the present—not the past—to forgive and ask forgiveness where necessary, and to show my appreciation for the love and time my parents invested in me. Trusting God for wisdom when conflicts arise, I want to make the time to maintain a good relationship with them so I will have no regrets—only sweet memories—when they're gone.

As a child of God I know I am complete in Him. He gives me everything I truly need, and everything He does, He does out of love. I want to know Him better every day and to become more like Him. So, trusting Him to help me make time, I commit myself to reading His Word regularly, talking with Him honestly, learning what pleases Him, and doing it.

As a sister to other women who know Christ, I appreciate the bond we have and the joy of doing things *together*. I'm grateful for the give-and-take of lifting one another's loads. So I commit myself to building relationships (not tearing others down), to looking for ways to encourage (not griping about something done differently than I would have done), and to developing a sensitivity to others' needs (not being so wrapped up in my own schedule and problems).

As a servant I am so grateful for all that Christ has done for me, that I want to serve Him by serving others. I enjoy the good feeling it gives me inside. I choose to give up my "rights" when necessary in order to meet someone else's need, and I pray for farsightedness that sees beyond my own four walls to the concerns of others.

As an adventurer in the kingdom I choose to seek first God's kingdom and His righteousness, trusting Him to provide my daily needs. I commit myself to Jesus' last desire as He left this earth—that we tell others about Him. And I trust Him to help me find the wholeness of purpose the Great Commission gives me in all my other responsibilities.

As one who sees the years slipping by too quickly, I want to concentrate on what will matter for eternity. I choose to focus less on physical than on spiritual maturity—which only gets better with age. As I read God's Word and talk everything over with Him, I can trust the Lord for strength and endurance when the body won't do all it once did. I choose to replace unhealthy concerns about appearance with a confident assurance that the fruit of His Spirit (love, joy, peace, patience, kindness, goodness, faithfulness, gentleness, and self-control) will shine through in a beauty that attracts others to Him.

Overall, trust in God and commitment are the keys here. Our pastor, Joel Johnson, says, "Immature people base actions on feelings instead of commitments." As mature women who love God, we need to polish our commitments—to Him, to our marriages, to our families, and to all our other relationships. It's surprising how freeing commitment can be!

Balancing Our Bonnets "Grace-fully"

What do we do with all these hats? There's a story in the Old Testament that I think we can translate into our struggles with our leaning tower of hats. God asked Moses to lead His people out of Egypt, but Moses didn't think he could handle all the responsibility.

"What is in your hand?" God asked.

Moses held up his dry old walking stick and shrugged. But when he yielded that old stick of God's creation to his own Creator, the Lord showed him how to use it to bring God glory.

I think the Lord asks us the same thing, but perhaps we can paraphrase the question this way: What is on your head? What hats are you wearing? God put them there—unless we've been window shopping again. And if we quit panicking and fretting about how we're going to get everything done and trust Him for *His* ultimate purpose for our lives, He'll show us how to wear all our hats—at the right times—with style!

So how do we view our many hats? As a nuisance? A burden? Something that keeps us from doing what we really want to do? Or do we see them as gifts and opportunities for service to our King and His kingdom?

It's easy to get bogged down with the scheduled rush, the tyranny of the present. But God never intended our service for

Him to be drudgery. He offers us His resources of faith, confidence, and strength so we can honor our commitments, strike a healthy balance, and persevere in all life's demands.

Panic perpetuates itself, but trusting God calms us with His confidence. Worry and trusting God are mutually exclusive.

Recently a number of verses I've known for a long time came together to provide a new perspective for me:

• Without God I can do nothing (John 15:5).

• With Him nothing is impossible (Luke 1:37).

• I can do all things through Christ, who strengthens me (Philippians 4:13).

• I am the Lord's servant. I will do what He asks me to do (Luke 1:38).

• I will see God work if I do not give up (Galatians 6:9).

• Above all, my confidence is this: He who began a good work in me will finish it (Philippians 1:6).

If Something's Gotta Go

I once heard a speaker (I wish I could remember who) say that we are the same people today that we were twenty years ago except for the books we read and the people we meet. I would add "and the choices we make." Today's advertising and cultural expectations cry out that we, as women, can have it all. Some modify that, saying we can have it all but not at the same time. But I don't think that's even necessarily true. Our choices are what make us unique.

Jean Bracken says she tries to balance her life by carefully evaluating her choices. Before she takes on another responsibility, she asks herself, "What will I have to give up to do this?"

I tend to take on something new, certain I can handle it, but later I have to pull an all-nighter or ask someone to bail me out at the last minute. My husband says he sees *some* progress in this area, though, however slow it may seem.

Making the tough choices and knowing what to let go is a continual challenge, isn't it? One woman says that when she and her husband became part of a new church she became overinvolved because she wanted to be loved and accepted. "Soon I was stretched out like an old sock," she says. When both family and church leadership urged her to cut back, she did. She passed some responsibilities on to competent successors but other ministries are dying that shouldn't, she says. "It's hard for me not to charge in and rescue them."

Those kinds of decisions require lots of prayer. When the Lord leads us to put some hats away, we need to commit them to His hands and not get in there and meddle. Quite often He has a larger purpose in mind that may even call for the death of a pet project.

But when we decide something's gotta go, we need to be careful what we throw out. Most women I know say the first thing they let slide is the housework. They make me feel so much better! Colleen—a wife, mother, and nurse, who is also involved in several activities at church—admits she's a perfectionist housekeeper. But, she says, "I've had to lower my cleanliness standards. Either that or drive myself totally crazy!"

Obviously we want to create a healthy environment to live in, but, as my grandma used to say, "*A little* dirt never hurt anybody." I personally have come to believe that a thin layer of dust gives furniture a kind of dreamlike aura.

One woman talks about a program in her community that supports women in their many roles. "It meets often and they encourage regular attendance," she says. "But I felt I needed to use that time *with* my family instead of meeting with other women to *talk about my family.*"

Kathy says that people often ask her how she keeps up with her teaching responsibilities, household chores, kids' sporting events, Sunday school teaching, and a myriad of other involvements. "I make sure I get enough sleep," she says. "I can't pull all-nighters as some people do."

Don't Throw Out the Counterweights

We need to be careful when we're deciding which hats to retire (at least for a time), so that we don't give up the things that help us maintain our balance.

While celebrating my premenopausal years by going back to school, I had to let almost everything else go. But two of the things I missed most were music (singing in our church choir) and needlework. Funny how I didn't miss the housework!

When I lost my office job and returned to working at home, I realized how much I needed people around me. Some individuals draw energy from solitude. I get mine from being with others. So even when nearing deadline on this book—when I was tempted to push myself to write night and day—I made myself get out for an evening of crafts one week and a dessert meeting the next. And I still made my deadline!

Ultimately, our Enemy tries to convince us that when we're overscheduled we don't have time to spend reading God's Word and praying in a one-on-one time with God. But I've found that when I carve out that time, somehow the important work still gets done. And my time alone with God is precious. That's what gives me the strength and wisdom to deal with all my other responsibilities.

Time Wasters or Mind Savers

Several years ago I picked up a book called *How to Get Control of Your Time and Your Life*. Several people told me that book had changed their lives. So I eagerly plopped down my quarter at the garage sale and took home my treasure. But, alas, I can't get control of my time and my life long enough to read it. So it sits in my stack of books to read—someday.

But everything I *have* managed to read about time management encourages us to identify the time wasters in our lives. I'll admit this is a good idea. I know television is one of mine. The TV set was virtually my teething ring, and though it is a good way to relax sometimes, I constantly fight with how much is too much.

I've identified a few other time wasters, too, but I once read a short article suggesting twenty things you can do during those precious seconds your food is in the microwave. Oh, please! Such micromanagement of our time explains burnout! Some *man* must have thought of that one! Farmers know they need to allow their land to lie fallow periodically so it can rest and rejuvenate. And what lovely gifts even those microwave-waiting seconds give our minds to meander, rest, and reflect.

Colleen says she's learning to take time for herself purposely, "to see the beauty of the little things around me, to rest and reflect."

Beauty in Working Together

But what about when we can't handle all our hats, when—despite our best balancing efforts—the pile is teetering and our lovely bonnets begin tumbling down all around us?

Carol, a gotta-be-involved-in-everything person, admits she gives everything she does 100 percent and tries to wear just one hat at a time. But, she says, sometimes it's a challenge "just to keep my head on."

When we're in over our heads, we need to holler for help! First to God, then to our families, but also to our sisters—and brothers—in Christ. A divorced friend of mine frequently mentions how important it is for her to have male input to help her keep perspective. One or two men in her church act as a sounding board and offer counsel when she needs it. What good balance!

Several months ago my husband and I enjoyed a Minnesota Orchestra concert featuring a cello soloist. (I used to play cello in my adolescent years, and I still melt at its rich, mellow tones.) That night we witnessed an amazing sight. When the soloist came to a passage calling for *forte pizzicato*, he plucked the string so vigorously that it snapped, yet he kept playing with only three strings. Instantly the second-chair cellist picked up her instrument, walked over to the soloist, and exchanged cellos with him. All the while, the orchestra continued playing, and the soloist hardly missed a beat.

As the second-chair cellist returned to her seat, the woman next to her handed her an extra string. Within seconds Ms. Second-Chair installed the string, imperceptibly tuned the instrument close to her ear, and returned the cello to its master—again hardly missing a beat.

It all happened so quickly and so smoothly that I don't think many people noticed. I couldn't help but think of how beautifully that illustrates the way we, as women, can work together to keep our lives moving. When one needs help another steps in to encourage, support, and even sometimes help her "stay in tune." No one remembers the name of the second-chair cellist in the Minnesota Orchestra (except friends and family, of course). But I, for one, will never forget her selfless act that kept the music flowing.

And wasn't it great that she didn't point and taunt, "Look, he broke a string!"

Above all, however, a 500-hats woman needs to be:

- joyful in hope
- patient in affliction
- faithful in prayer (Romans 12:12).

Dorothy, a retired but perpetually busy grandmother, says, "I am learning more every day that lifting up my children, their mates, and our grandchildren in prayer is the greatest gift I can give them. It also binds me closer to them than any one thing I can do."

There is nothing that binds people together in a more intimate relationship than praying for one another. It's difficult to be judgmental of another woman's choice of hats or the way she wears them when we're praying for her.

In Front of the Fitting Room Mirror

The Bible says it's healthy to stand in front of the fitting room mirror to assess our lives—where we are, what we're doing, how we're thinking, where we're going. But we're supposed to pay attention to what we see and make the necessary adjustments. The mirror that helps us keep an eye on all our roles as women is God's Word (see James 1:23-25).

The world around us screams so many demanding messages about looks, fulfillment, attitude, and success. But God speaks quietly as we read His Word. We need to look intently at Scripture, the perfect law that gives true freedom (v. 25) and "continue to do so." And then if we don't forget what we've seen and heard but make the necessary adjustments, God will bless us in what we do. We have His Word on it!

As we stand before the mirror of God's Word, we can assess each hat we wear—each role we serve—making sure it's *from* Him, and committing it *to* Him. Just as little Bartholomew Cubbins handed his most beautiful of all hats to his king, we can commit our entire millinery collection into *our* King's hands, asking Him to help us manage all our many hats well.

With thankful hearts we can look to the Lord and say,

> Lord, this is where You've put me.
> These are the hats You've given me.
> Help me to wear them fashionably,
> not complaining,
> but bringing honor and glory to You!

Study Questions

1. Read James 1:23-25. James likens the Scriptures to what essential makeup case item? What important point does he make here?

2. Read Exodus 3:1-12 and 4:1-5. God called Moses to a great leadership task. What did Moses have to do to be convinced that God was in control?

3. Read Ephesians 2:8-10. Many times a woman compares herself with other women and comes away with either low self-esteem or pride. Why do you think God didn't base our salvation on our works or how many hats we wear or how well we juggle all our responsibilities? What does verse 10 have to say about our roles and actions?

4. Read Matthew 6:33. When the world around us dictates what we have to give up if we want to get ahead, how does this verse help us keep life in perspective?

5. Read Exodus 20:1-6. What characteristic that we usually think of as sin is here attributed to God? We know God is holy and pure and has no sin, so how do you reconcile those two thoughts? How might some of the hats we wear become idols in our lives?

6. Read Romans 12:12. What are some characteristics that a woman of 500 hats (more or less) needs to keep going on the days those hats weigh heavy on her head?

7. Read and then write down the essence of the following verses: John 15:5, Luke 1:37, Philippians 4:13, Luke 1:38, Galatians 6:9, and Philippians 1:6. For example, for John 15:5 you might write, "Without God I can do nothing." How do you think these verses can help us maintain a proper view of our many hats?

(You may want to write or type these on an index card that you can place on your bathroom mirror or over the kitchen sink as a reminder.)

The 500-Hats Woman's Prayer for Her Sisters in Christ

We have not stopped praying for you and asking God to fill you with the knowledge of his will through all spiritual wisdom and understanding. And we pray this in order that you may live a life worthy of the Lord and may please him in every way: bearing fruit in every good work, growing in the knowledge of God, being strengthened with all power according to his glorious might so that you may have great endurance and patience, and joyfully giving thanks to the Father, who has qualified you to share in the inheritance of the saints in the kindom of light. For he has rescued us from the dominion of darkness and brought us into the kingdom of the Son he loves, in whom we have redemption, the forgiveness of sins.

COLOSSIANS 1:9-14

Notes

Introduction

1. You owe it to yourself to read or reread Dr. Seuss' inimitably entertaining rendition of this old English folktale. Dr. Seuss, *The 500 Hats of Bartholomew Cubbins* (New York: Random House, 1989 reissue edition).

Chapter One

1. Ruth Senter, *Have We Really Come a Long Way?* (Minneapolis: Bethany House, 1997), 14.
2. John Gray, *Men Are from Mars, Women Are from Venus* (New York: HarperCollins, 1992), 10.

Chapter Four

1. "The Balancing Act," *Ladies' Home Journal,* October 1997, 68.
2. Karen Scalf Linamen and Linda Holland, *Working Women, Workable Lives* (Wheaton, Ill.: Harold Shaw, 1993), 173.
3. Elizabeth Ritchie Johnson, "I Couldn't Afford My Job," *Redbook,* April 1991, 90.
4. Deborah Fallows, "When Both Parents Work," *People,* July 1987, 42.
5. Larry Burkett, *Women Leaving the Workplace* (Chicago: Moody, 1995), 20–21.

Chapter Five

1. Lois Duncan, "When Your Husband's Relatives Drive You Crazy," *Woman's Day,* March 7, 1989, 64.
2. Anonymous author, "My In-Laws Wouldn't Leave Us Alone," *Good Housekeeping,* May 1983, 38.

Chapter Seven

1. Donna Partow, *No More Lone Ranger Moms* (Minneapolis: Bethany House, 1995), 18.
2. Contact *Pursuit* magazine at 901 E. 78th St., Minneapolis, MN, 55420-1360 or (612) 853-1750 for sample copy and ordering information.

Chapter Eight

1. Marcia L. Mitchell, *Giftedness: Discovering Your Areas of Strength* (Minneapolis: Bethany House, 1988, currently out of print), 37–38.